CAROLS

*Their Origin, Music, and Connection
with Mystery-Plays*

SALVATOR · MUNDI ·
· NATUS · EST

FMR

CAROLS

Their Origin, Music, and Connection with Mystery-Plays

By

WILLIAM J. PHILLIPS

Mus. Doc., Queen's College, Oxford

With a Foreword by
SIR FREDERICK BRIDGE

GREENWOOD PRESS, PUBLISHERS
WESTPORT, CONNECTICUT

Originally published in 1921
by George Routledge & Sons, Ltd., London
and E. P. Dutton & Company, New York

First Greenwood Reprinting 1970

Library of Congress Catalogue Card Number 75-109821

SBN 8371-4312-8

Printed in the United States of America

FOREWORD

I have read Dr. Phillips' little Carol Book with great interest. He seems to have explored in many directions, and the examples given of some of the old carols are quite new to me.

There is hardly a place of worship—Cathedral, Church, or Chapel—in which carols are not sung. But when I was young it was a very rare thing to hear them sung in Church.

I remember the Rev. Thomas Helmore (who did a really great work in bringing to the notice of Church people these delightful old things) lecturing on the subject, and it fell to my lot as organist of a country church to perform some of his selections. Since then I have always taken much interest in the subject, and at Westminster Abbey I was able to establish carol services at Christmas which have been among the most largely attended of any special services. And again, at the Royal Albert Hall, the Royal Choral Society has given a yearly carol concert which is one of the most popular of the series given by the Society. Dr. Phillips' book will help those who desire to select *real* carols.

The carol has a character of its own—it is not a part-song or a hymn tune, but something quite distinct. There are some good modern carols, of course, but a good old one is to be preferred.

FOREWORD

I think this little book will help in this direction, and I am glad to have this opportunity of recommending it.

J. FREDERICK BRIDGE.

Cloisters, Westminster Abbey.

PREFACE

This book is the outcome of a series of lectures given by the writer at various times on the subject of Carols and their music, and is published at the request of many friends who wished for a more permanent record than memory could afford.

The subject is so fascinating and so little has been done to popularize it that the author hopes that the present volume may be of general interest, and for this purpose it has been written in a simple style, without technicalities.

The amount of Carol material is so large that only a comparatively small selection could be inserted, but it is believed to be sufficiently varied to illustrate the many types which exist and to give some idea of the popularity of the Carol in days of old. If this book serves to awaken in the reader an interest in the rich store of carol literature which we inherit from our forefathers, it will amply repay the author for his work. It only remains for the writer to gratefully acknowledge his indebtedness to Dr. Ralph Dunstan for his assistance and kindness in correcting the proofs.

W. J. PHILLIPS.

CONTENTS

CONTENTS

CONTENTS

What sweeter music can we bring
Than a carol for to sing
The birth of this our Heavenly King?

HERRICK.

LIST OF ILLUSTRATIONS

ORIGIN OF CAROLS AND MYSTERY-PLAYS

The very first carol ever heard by mortal ears was that which was sung by the angels over the fields of Bethlehem when our Lord was born, " Glory be to God on high, and on earth peace, goodwill towards men," and although we can quite well imagine St. Mary crooning a cradle-song over her little Babe in the Bethlehem manger, yet it was not until more than 1200 years later that the first carol was sung on earth in a tiny Italian village, called Grecia, near Assisi. Here it was that that great mystic of the Middle Ages, St. Francis of Assisi, made the first Christmas crèche or crib, and the brethren of his community sang Christmas hymns in honour of the birth of the Saviour of the world. The origin of the carol and crèche of St. Françis was on this wise :—During the eleventh and twelfth centuries there existed in the Christian Church a great heresy called Manicheism. It originated in the east, and was brought over from Asia Minor into Bulgaria by the Paulicians in the ninth century, and spread from there over the whole of Southern Europe. This heresy denied the

Virgin Birth of Christ, and was directly antagonistic to the Church's doctrine of the Incarnation. The Manicheans asserted that all matter was evil and only things of the spirit good, that the entrance of the spirit into relation with the body brought about the fall of man, and that salvation could only be attained by emancipating the soul from the bonds of the flesh. The doctrine of the Incarnation could have no place in such a religion, and it was in order to combat this then so prevalent heresy that St. Francis cast about in his mind for some way of popularising in the minds of the people a knowledge and true understanding of the meaning of the Incarnation. A practical way of embodying his idea came to him when he was journeying from Rome in the year 1223 to stay over Christmastide at Grecia, near Assisi. Accordingly, on his arrival at Grecia, having obtained permission, he caused a manger, an ox, an ass, and all the trappings of a stable to be prepared in the Church, and according to Mrs. Oliphant, in her " Francis of Assisi,"* " Francis and his brethren arranged these things into a visible representation of the occurrences of the night at Bethlehem. It was a reproduction, so far as they knew how, in startling realistic detail of the surroundings of the first Christmas. . . . The population of the neighbourhood rose as one man to the call of St. Francis. They gathered round the village Church with tapers and torches, making luminous

---

* " Francis of Assisi " (chapter xiv.) by Mrs. Oliphant. *Macmillan & Co.*

the December night. The brethren within the Church, and the crowds of the faithful who came and went with their lights, in and out of the darkness, poured out their hearts in praises to God ; and the friars sang *new canticles*, which were listened to with all the eagerness of a people accustomed to wandering jongleurs and minstrels, and to whom such songs were all the food to be had for the intellect and imagination. . . . We are told that Francis stood by this, his simple theatrical representation (for such, indeed, it was, no shame to him) all the night long, sighing for joy and filled with unspeakable sweetness. His friend Giovanni, looking on, had a vision while he stood apart, gazing and wondering at the saint. Giovanni saw, or dreamed, that a beautiful infant—a child dead or in a trance—lay in the manger which he had himself prepared, and that, as Francis bent over the humble bed, the Babe slowly awoke, and stretched out its arms towards him. It was the child Christ, dead in the hearts of a careless people, dead or lost in the slumber of a wicked world, but waking up to new life, and kindling the whole slumberous universe around him at the touch and breath of that supreme love which was in his servant's heart." This simple performance in a tiny Italian village was the origin not only of the Christmas carol, but also of the Christmas Mystery-Plays. The Crèche, Crib, or Praesepio, of St. Francis, can be seen in many Churches at Christmastide to this day, while the singing of carols still flourishes and tends to grow more popular as time goes on.

The only break in the continuity of carol singing in this country occurred during the period of the Reformation. We owe to the Reformers not only the despoiling and whitewashing of our Churches, the breaking up and removal of the organs, etc., but also the suppression of Christmas carols and all Christmas festivities, and even an attempt to suppress Christmas itself!

The last Wednesday in the month was kept by them as a Fast-day, and because in the year 1644 Christmas Day happened to fall on the last Wednesday in the month, the people were ordered to keep it as a Fast! And in the year 1652 Parliament even went so far as to order that " no observation shall be had of the 25th of December, commonly called Christmas Day." No services were allowed in the Churches on that day, and Evelyn, the diarist, and others were arrested for committing a breach of the ordinance of Parliament by receiving the Holy Communion on Christmas morning. Our forefathers, as freedom-loving as ourselves, rebelled against such interference with their liberties, and it was not long before they demanded and recovered their ancient winter festival, and with it a revival of the carols.

This decline of carolry in the 17th century is shown by the contents of a curious old book, now in the British

Museum. It was published in 1642, and bears the following quaint title :—

Psalms and Songs of Sion.
Turned into the language
and set to the tunes of
a strange land by
W. S.
Intended for Christmas Carols,
And fitted to divers of the most noted
and common but solemn tunes,
Everywhere in this land familiarly
used and known.

The initials " W. S." stand for William Slater, and upon the copy of this book some former possessor has written the names of some of the tunes to which the author designed his Psalms to be sung, e.g. :—

Psalm 8 to the tune " Jane Shore."
     ,,   19   ,,   " Foster's Dreame."
     ,,   43   ,,   " Crimson Velvet."
     ,,   47   ,,   " Garden Green."
     ,,   84   ,,   " The Fairest Nymph of the
                              Valley."

Hone says :—" This adaptation of religious poetry to secular melody in England is noticed by Shakespeare in the " Winter Tale " (in Act 4, Scene 3), where the clown relates that his sister, being the mistress at his father's shearing-feast, made four-and-twenty nosegays for the sheep shearers, all good catch singers, with but one Puritan among them, and *he sings psalms to hornpipes.*"

That such concoctions should be called carols shows how low the art of carolling had descended, and it seems obvious that under the gloomy conditions imposed by the *Puritans*, the suppression of Christmas revelry, and the almost extinction of libraries, the clock of artistic progress was set back for many a long year. With the exception of a few on the story of the Shepherds, which were doubtless inspired by the craze for pastorals prevalent at the time, very few carols of any great merit appear to have been written during the period of the Reformation. Those to the Virgin and the Saints were, of course, banned as prelatical, and the result was the closing of one of the chief sources of the inspiration of the earlier poets.

The Elizabethan poets contented themselves with pastorals and hymn-like compositions which have little of the religious fervour of the older carols. One has only to compare Jeremy Taylor's "Hymn for Christmas Day," one of his *Festival Hymns*, with the old carol, "When Christ was born of Mary free" (written about 1500), at once to perceive the difference in style and quality.

Hymn for Christmas Day.
Jeremy Taylor (1613-1667).
(A dialogue between three shepherds.)

Where is this blessed Babe
That hath made
All the world so full of joy
And expectation ;
That glorious Boy
That crowns each nation
With a triumphant wreath of blessedness ?

Where should He be but in the throng
And among
His angel ministers that sing
And take wing
Just as may echo to His voice,
And rejoice
When wing and tongue and all
May so procure their happiness ?

But He hath other waiters now,
A poor cow,
An ox and mule, stand and behold,
And wonder
That a stable should enfold
Him that can thunder.

Chorus : Oh, what a gracious God have we,
How good ! How great ! even as our misery.

Now compare this with the following lovely old carol written about 1500, and the difference of quality and style will be apparent at once :—

When Christ was born of Mary free,
In Bethlehem that fair city,
Angels did sing with mirth and glee,
    In excelsis gloria.

Herdsmen beheld those angels bright,
To them appearing with great light,
And said, " God's Son is born this night,
    In excelsis gloria.

This King is come to save mankind,
As in Scriptures we do find,
Therefore this song have we in mind,
    In excelsis gloria.

Then, O Lord, for Thy great grace,
Grant us the bliss to see Thy face,
That we may sing to Thy solace
    In excelsis gloria.

Of course, there were exceptions, as, for example, Robert Herrick's beautiful " Ode on the Birth of our Saviour," one of his *Noble Numbers*, written in 1647.

An Ode to the Birth of Our Saviour.

In numbers, and but these few,
I sing Thy birth, O Jesu!
Thou pretty Baby, born here
With sup'rabundant scorn here,
Who for Thy princely port here,
 Hadst for Thy place
 Of birth a base
Out-stable for Thy court here.

Instead of neat enclosures
Of interwoven osiers,
Instead of fragrant posies
Of daffodils and roses,
Thy cradle, kingly stranger,
 As Gospel tells,
 Was nothing else
But here a homely manger.

But we with silks, not crewels,
With sundry precious jewels,
And lily-work, will dress Thee ;
And as we dispossess Thee
Of clouts, we'll make a chamber,
 Sweet babe, for Thee
 Of ivory,
And plastered round with amber.

The Jews they did disdain Thee,
But we will entertain Thee
With glories to await here
Upon Thy princely state here,
And more for love than pity,
  From year to year
  We'll make Thee here
A freeborn of our city.

But with some few exceptions, from about the latter
half of the seventeenth century, and during the eighteenth
and nineteenth century, the art of carol writing de-
clined, in spite of the power of the printing press in
producing broadsheet publications, which were popular
with the people, and helped to preserve many versions
of old carols which would have otherwise been lost for
ever. It is only in recent years that some of our best
lyrical writers, such as William Morris, Christina Rossetti,
A. C. Swinburne, R. L. Gales, and others have attempted
to produce carols in the old style, with excellent results.
A beautiful specimen is Swinburne's " Three damsels in
the Queen's Chamber," an illustration of which, designed
by Sidney Meteyard, is reproduced here.

Three Damsels in the Queens Chamber

Three Damsels in the Queens Chamber
The Queens mouth was most fair
She spake a word of Gods mother
As the comb went in her hair
Mary that is of might,
Bring us to thy Sons sight.

CAROLS AND DANCING

It is not generally known that carolling was formerly identified with dancing as well as singing. In this the word " Carol " shows an interesting parallel with the word " Ballad," for although both these names are now used to denote song, originally both implied dancing, as well as singing.

In the Paradiso (Canto xxiv., v. 17) Dante uses the word " Carola " as meaning a singing-dance :—

E come cerchi in tempra d'orinoli
Si giran si che il primo, a chi pon mente
Quieto pare, e l'ultimo che voli :
Cosi quelle *carole* differente-mente danzando, della
sua richezza
Mi si facean stimar, veloci e lente.

And as the wheels in works of horologes
Revolve so that the first to the beholder
Motionless seems, and the last one to fly,
So in like manner did these *carols*, dancing
In different measure, of their affluence
Give me the gauge, as they were swift or slow.
(*Longfellow's translation*).

(12)

And dear old Chaucer sometimes implies dancing, and sometimes singing, as in the " Dreame " :—

> " I saw her daunce so comely,
> Carol and sing so sweetly."

Then, again, beautiful illustrations of carolling may be seen in the paintings of Fra Angelico, where the Christmas angels not only sing, but dance as well, while the angels in Botticelli's Nativity picture in the National Gallery are veritable pictures of poetry in motion. In old French " Carole " signified a dance in a ring. This dance was accompanied by singing, the name was perpetuated by the song, and became incorporated into most of the Western European languages.

The famous Stonehenge in Wiltshire was also known as Choir-gaur, the Giants' Dance or " Carol " (probably from the rings of stones resembling dancers), and is mentioned in the Harding Chronicles : " Within the Giants' Carole, they so hight, the Stone-hengles that now so namèd been." This combined dancing and singing existed among pre-Christian peoples from time immemorial, the Romans having their religious dances like the Druids, and there seems no doubt that it found its way from pagan ritual into the Christian Church. Once established, dancing became immensely popular and caused many scandals, so much so, that we find the 3rd Council of Toledo in the year 589 forbidding dancing in churches on the Vigils of Saints' days, and the Council of Avignon in 1209 placing a similar restriction on the performance in churches of theatrical dances and songs. But these popular customs were far too deeply rooted to be easily suppressed, and religious dances have persisted until comparatively recent times. Up to the 17th century the apprentices were accustomed to dance in the nave of York Minster on Shrove Tuesday, and Krier, in " Die Springprocession in Echternach," gives an interesting account of a dancing procession, called " Die springende Heiligen " (the jumping saints), which take place every Tuesday in Whitsun week at Echternach in Luxembourg, where the clergy, choir, and people, all dance to the church and round the altar, singing carols. In the Cathedral of Seville in Spain a religious dance is performed by the choir-boys three times a year, on Shrove Tuesday, the Feast of Corpus Christi, and the Feast of the Immaculate Conception.   The choir-boys, clad in antique Spanish costumes, group around the choir lectern, on which is the great illuminated music-book from which they sing their jubilant song, accompanied by an orchestra of stringed and wind instruments.   The singing being ended, the youngsters dance round the lectern, and before the high altar.   At the end of the dance the boys form in line and perform a brilliant fantasy on their castanets ; twice again the whole performance is gone through (three times in all), the little fellows then file solemnly out of the choir, and the service is ended. Such a performance in an English church would shock our ideas of the fitness of things, but in Seville, with its almost Oriental splendour of architecture and colouring, its Moorish gateways, orange groves, and general extra-European atmosphere, it all seems quite natural and appropriate.

MYSTERY-PLAYS

The Christmas Plays, of which St. Francis' simple
tableaux were the forerunners, were *acted* versions of
the Christmas scenes. These old Mystery and Miracle
Plays were very helpful to the Church in teaching people
at a time when few could read, by the acting of Bible
stories before them. They were originally performed by
the clergy themselves, and given in Latin, and as women
were not allowed to appear on the stage, their parts
were also taken by the priests. All sorts of secular
elements soon crept into the Miracle and Mystery-Plays
when they passed later into the hands of the people
themselves. Comic scenes and buffoonery of the most
vulgar sort became very popular, and the most important
person in the Miracle-Plays was often the devil, who
generally played the part of a clown or fool. Mr. Brand
says that the rank of the audiences attests the celebrity
of these performances. In 1483 Richard the Third
visited Coventry to see the Corpus Christi plays, and in
1492 they were attended by Henry the Seventh and his
Queen, who highly commended them. For a long time
the most popular of these early festival performances
were " La Fête de Foux " and " La Fête de L'Ane."

The " Fête de Foux " (or Feast of Fools) was performed at the Feast of the Circumcision (New Year's Eve and Day), and the "Fête de L'Ane" (or Donkey's Festival) at Christmas. The Feast of Fools was, at first, associated with the Church, but later it became so vulgar that it developed into a regular Saturnalia, something like the ancient festival of Pagan Rome. Bishop Grosseteste condemned it in the 13th century, and it died out in England at the end of the 14th century. The "Fête de L'Ane" does not appear to have been known in England, but at Beauvais, where a gorgeous performance was carried out (in commemoration of the Flight into Egypt), a donkey was dressed in handsome clothing, and a young girl rode on its back, carrying a child in her arms, to the Church, where the following old Latin Prose, " Orientis Partibus," was sung, followed by noises imitative of the braying of an ass.

O..ri...en.tis par..ti....bus, Ad.ven...ta.vit as.in....us,

Pul.cher et for...tis.si....mus, Sar.cin.....is ap...tis..si...mus.

Hez. sire As.nez. Hez!

Many readers will be interested to note that this old tune has come down to us, and is still popular, being

sung in many Churches at the present day to the hymn,
" Soldiers who are Christ's below," but in common time
instead of triple time.

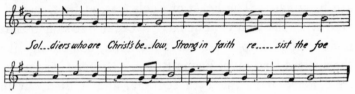

Sol...diers who are Christ's be...low, Strong in faith re.......sist the foe

Boundless is the pledged re...ward, Un...to them that serve the Lord.

By the Fifteenth Century there were three distinct
forms of these histrionic representations: The Mystery-
Play, dealing with the events in the Life of Christ ;
the Miracle-Play, representing the doings of the Saints ;
and the Morality-Play, in which were shown allegorical
representations of various virtues and vices.   They were
exceedingly popular in this country in the Middle Ages,
being generally performed in the open air on specially
erected stages.   Four whole collections of Mystery-Plays
have come down to us, viz. :—The York and the Townley Plays, and the Chester and Coventry Plays.   The
oldest of these are the York Plays, next come the
Townley Plays in the Fourteenth Century, with the Coventry last of all in the Fifteenth or Sixteenth Century.
Each play was performed by members of a particular
Trading Company, such as the Glovers', the Tailors',
or the Fishers' Company.   Every Company had its
own pageant cart on which they performed.   These
pageant carts or scaffolds were on four wheels, and were

divided horizontally by the platform or stage into two sections. In the lower half, screened from the public view, the actors dressed themselves, and then afterwards acted their parts in the upper section, which was open to the view like a modern stage. The costumes were curious. All the characters representing Divine and Sacred persons had their hair and beards gilded. Herod was clad as a Saracen, while the demons wore hideous heads, and the " souls " black and white coats, according to their kind and destination. The angels had gold skins and wings !*

There were two sorts of performances, the fixed-stage to which the audience went to see the plays, and the Processional plays, in which a series of Pageants pass d in procession, such as those performed at the Corpus Christi Festival. The fixed-stage performance was most popular on the Continent, and the Processional play in England. The Corpus Christi Festival was instituted in 1264, and its procession soon became a splendid and popular spectacle. Various scenes representing the religious history of mankind were performed by the various Guilds. As a rule, each Guild produced the story most nearly allied in character to its trade. The Goldsmiths, for instance, played " The Adoration of the Magi," and offered gold, frankincense, and myrrh ; the Boatmen and Boatbuilders produced " The Ark."

The writers of these old plays seem to have had a

* Encyclopædia Britt.

good eye for stage effect, for they frequently introduced
a sort of comic man, one of the Vices, or the Devil,
apparently as a relief to the more serious characters.
In one old play mentioned by Mr. Bullen four of the
characters were Saint George, The Turk, the Doctor,
and Beelzebub ! Mr. Beelzebub comes on the stage
grotesquely apparelled, carrying a club under his arm,
and a tin pail under his chin, and introduces himself to
the audience with the following curious lines :—

> Here come I, Beelzebub ;
> Under my arm I carry a club,
> Under my chin I carry a pan,
> Don't I look a nice young man ?

A very nice young man, no doubt ! For the character
portrayed in Beelzebub was a lesson to the beholders.
The club he carried signified brutality and murder, and
the pan greed. A *very* nice young man indeed !

Noah's wife also figures as a favourite comic character
in several of these old plays, and a very natural human
touch is shown in one where Mrs. Noah refuses to enter
the Ark without the rest of her family relations ! And
St. Joseph, although he is described in a very gentle
manner in the York plays, in the Townley Mysteries is
treated rather humorously. After he has been told by
the Angel to take the young Child and his mother and
flee into Egypt he complains of the troubles his marriage
has brought him, and (confidentially, in an aside to the
audience) he advises the young people not to marry !

The accounts for the cost of the production are decidedly amusing. In " The Introduction to the English Drama " in the " Cambridge History of English Literature " the following curious items are mentioned :

Paid for making 3 worlds .. .. 3 pence.
Two yards and a half of buckram
    for the Holy Ghost's coat .. 2s. 1d.

Other properties mentioned are " Hell-mouth and the Head of a Whale, with jaws worked by two men, out of which devil-boys ran."

But there are many quaint and charming scenes in the Christmas Mysteries, as in the Coventry Pageant (1468) performed by the Company of " Sheremen and Taylors " on the festival of Corpus Christi, where the Shepherds bring their homely gifts to the Christ-Child.

The first shepherd, offering his pipe to Him, says :—

I have nothing to present with thy Child
But my pipe. (Hold ! hold ! take it in Thy hand !)
Wherein much pleasure that I have found.
And now to honour Thy glorious birth
Thou shalt have it to make Thee mirth.

A second shepherd gives his hat, and says :—

Hold ! take thou, here, my hat on Thy head,
And now of one thing, Thou art well sped,
For weather Thou hast now no need to complain,
For wind, nor sun, hail, snow or rain.

The third shepherd presents the Child with his mittens, saying :—

> Hail be Thou ! Lord over water and lands !
> For Thy coming we all may make mirth.
> Have here my mittens to put on Thy hands,
> Other treasure have I none to present Thee with.

A similar scene is enacted in the York Mysteries (see page 106), except that in the latter play the shepherds' presents are a brooch, cobnuts, and a horn spoon !

One Miracle-Play, " The Creation of the World," was perhaps as popular as any of these, and was acted in London as late as the reign of Queen Anne.   The Hand-bill of the performance is as follows :—

BY HER MAJESTIE'S PERMISSION.

At Heatly's Booth,

Over against the Cross Daggers, next to Mr. Miller's Booth :

During the time of Bartholomew fair, will be presented a little Opera, called The Old Creation of the World, newly reviv'd, with the addition of the Glorious Battle obtained over the French and Spaniards by his Grace the Duke of Marlborough.

The Contents are these.

1. The Creation of Adam and Eve.
2. The intreagues of Lucifer in the Garden of Eden.
3. Adam and Eve driven out of Paradise.
4. Cain going to plough, Abel driving sheep.

5. Cain killeth his brother Abel.
6. Abraham offering his son Isaac.
7. Three Wise Men of the East guided by a Star, who worship him.
8. Joseph and Mary flee away by night upon an ass.
9. King Herod's cruelty, his men's spears laden with children.
10. Rich Dives invites his friends, and orders his porter to keep the beggars from his gate.
11. Poor Lazarus comes a begging at rich Dives' gate, the dogs lick his sores.
12. The good angel and death contend for Lazarus' life.
13. Rich Dives is taken sick and dieth, he is buried in great solemnity.
14. Rich Dives in Hell, and Lazarus in Abraham's bosom, seen in a most glorious object, all in machines, descending in a throne, guarded with multitudes of angels, with the breaking of the clouds, discovering the palace of the Sun, in double and treble prospect, to the admiration of the spectators.

CONNECTION OF CAROLS WITH MYSTERY-PLAYS

At first carols were merely sung as Intermezzi between the scenes of the Mysteries, exactly in the same way as music is played between the acts of a modern drama ; but after a time these carol-interludes became so popular with the audience that there was often great rivalry between the actors and the carol-singers, and the audience, having taken a great liking to the carols, were always asking (like Oliver Twist) for more, and it is recorded that, at Chester, the audience once wrecked the stage and properties and beat the players because they did not get enough carols to please them ! By the thirteenth or fourteenth century, however, these difficulties were overcome, and the singers and players becoming incorporated, the music was performed on the stage as part of the play itself. Henceforth the musicians led the players. The organist was furnished with a little portable organ, which he carried fastened to his shoulders by a strap. Blowing the bellows with his left hand and playing the keys with his right (very much like a street-singer playing his accordion nowadays), he led the procession to and fro across the stage, followed by the singers. Sometimes the enthusiasm of the audience was so great that the procession marched into the street, and, joined by the audience, marched round the roads with the players, singing the carols. From this custom it was an easy step to the singing of the carols apart from the Mysteries, and by the fifteenth century it had become a common practice to sing the carols alone, without histrionic representation.

CAROLS OF
THE VIRGIN MARY

Among the Nativity carols are a large number which hymn the Virgin Mother herself. These are practically all pre-Reformation work, and many of them are of great beauty and rank with the best specimens of old English lyrics. Most of the earlier carols are macaronic, or composite, and have lines in English and Latin alternately, or end their stanzas with a Latin refrain, as does the old carol, "When Christ was born of Mary free" on page 8, where every verse ends with "*In excelsis gloria.*"

The following little fifteenth-century carol is written in English throughout and is a charming specimen :—

> I sing of a maid
>   That is makeless,
> King of all kings
>   To her Son she ches.*
>
> He came all so still
>   Where His mother was,
> As dew in April
>   That falleth on the grass.

* Chose.

He came all so still
    To His mother's bower,
As dew in April
    That falleth on the flower.

He came all so still
    Where His mother lay
As dew in April
    That falleth on the spray.

Mother and maiden
    Was never none but she ;
Well may such a lady
    Goddes mother be.

In many of these " Mary " Carols the Virgin is often likened to lilies and roses, as in the old fifteenth-century carol in a manuscript preserved in the library at Trinity College, Cambridge, where she is called a rose :—

There is no rose of such virtue
As is the Rose that bare Jesu.
        Alleluia.

For in this Rose contained was
Heaven and earth in little space
        Res Miranda!

By that Rose we well may see,
There be One God in Persons Three,
        Pares forma.

The angels sung the shepherds to
" *Gloria in excelsis Deo.*"

                    Gaudeamus.

Leave we all this worldly mirth,
And follow we this joyful birth,

                    Transeamus.

In others of these old carols Mary is sometimes also
represented as a bird, as in the following :—

As I lay upon a night,
My thought was on a bird so bright,
That men call Mary, full of might,

                    Redemptoris Mater.

Lo ! here came Gabriel with light,
And said, " Hail be thou, blissful wight
To be called now art thou dight

                    Redemptoris Mater.

At that word that Lady bright
Anon conceived God full of might ;
Then men wist well that she was hight

                    Redemptoris Mater.

When Jesus on the Rood was pight,
Mary was doleful of that sight
Till she saw Him rise upright,

                    Redemptoris Mater.

Jesus that sittest in heaven light,
Grant us to come before Thy sight
With that *bird* that is so bright,

                    Redemptoris Mater.

Amongst the many beautiful pre-Reformation carols on the Annunciation still existing is the following specimen, probably of fifteenth century origin. The curious geographical error in the first verse, where Gabriel is sent "*from Nazareth to a City of Galilee*," should be noted. In the version in Wright's "Songs and Carols," printed by the Percy Society, it reads, "By Gabriel to Nazareth, City of Galilee." The melody is given, with the words, in the original manuscript, together with the secular words of a drinking song (see page 104), which go to the same tune, the sacred words being probably sung in church and the secular elsewhere.

Nowell, Nowell, Nowell, Nowell.
This is the salutation of the Angel Gabriel.

1. Tidings true there be come new,
      Sent from the Trinity,
   By Gabriel from Nazareth,
      To city of Galilee ;
   A clean maiden, and pure virgin
      Through her humility
   Hath conceived the Person
      Second in Deity.

Nowell, Nowell, Nowell, Nowell.
This is the salutation of the Angel Gabriel.

2.   Whenas that he presented was
       Before her fair visage,
   With simple mien and goodly wise
       To her he did homage,
   And said, " Lady, from heaven high,
       The Lord his heritage,
   For He of thee now born will be,
       I come on His message."

       Nowell, Nowell, Nowell, Nowell.
   This is the salutation of the Angel Gabriel.

3.   " Hail Mary, news I bring to thee,
       I come from 'fore God's face,
   Hail, temple of the Deity !
       Hail, maiden full of grace !
   Hail, virgin pure ! I thee assure,
       Within a little space
   Thou shalt conceive, and Him receive,
       Who will bring great solace."

       Nowell, Nowell, Nowell, Nowell.
   This is the salutation of the Angel Gabriel.

4.   Then spake the Blessed Virgin then,
       And answered womanly :
   " Whate'er my Lord commandeth me,
       I will obey truly.
   Ecce sum humillima
       Ancilla Domini :
   Secundum verbum tuum
       Fiat mihi."

       Nowell, Nowell, Nowell, Nowell.
   This is the salutation of the Angel Gabriel.

THE NARRATIVE OR STORY-TELLING CAROLS

Many of the old carols are founded upon legends. Perhaps one of the most interesting of these is the "Cherry-tree" carol. The poem itself is probably eighteenth-century work, but the story is also to be found in the Coventry Mystery-Plays of the fifteenth century. The carol is in two parts, the second being the better. The first part takes the form of a dialogue between Mary and Joseph when on their way to Bethlehem before the birth of the Saviour. As they pass a tree loaded with cherries Mary has a great wish for some of the fruit, and requests Joseph to pluck some cherries for her, but Joseph brusquely refuses, whereupon the tree bows down and offers its fruit to her.

Joseph was an old man,
And an old man was he,
When he wedded sweet Mary
In the land of Galilee.

Joseph and Mary walked
Through an orchard good,
Where was berries and cherries
As red as any blood.

Joseph and Mary walked
Through an orchard green,
Where was berries and cherries
As thick as might be seen.

O then bespoke Mary,
So meek and so mild,
" Pluck me one cherry, Joseph,
For I am with child."

O then bespoke Joseph,
With words most unkind,
" Let him pluck thee a cherry
That brought thee with child."

O then bespake the babe
Within his mother's womb,
" Bow down then the tallest tree
For my mother to have some."

Then bowed down the highest tree
Unto his mother's hand.
Then cried she, " See, Joseph,
I have cherries at command."

O then bespake Joseph,
" I have done Mary wrong ;
But cheer up, my dearest,
And be not cast down.

O eat your cherries, Mary,
O eat your cherries now,
O eat your cherries, Mary,
That grow upon the bough."

Then Mary plucked a cherry,
As red as the blood ;
Then Mary went home
With her heavy load.

———

PART 2.

As Joseph was a-walking
He heard an angel sing :
" This night shall be born
Our heavenly King.

He neither shall be born
In housen nor in hall,
Nor in the place of Paradise,
But in an ox's stall.

He neither shall be clothed
In purple nor in pall,
But all in fair linen
As were babies all.

He neither shall be rocked
In silver nor in gold,
But in a wooden cradle
That rocks on the mould.

D

He neither shall be christened
In white wine nor red,
But with fair spring water
With which we were christened."

———

PART 3.

Then Mary took her young son
And set him on her knee :
" I pray thee, now, dear child,
Tell how this world shall be."

" O I shall be as dead, mother,
As the stones in the wall ;
O the stones in the streets, mother,
Shall mourn for me all.

Upon Easter Day, mother,
My uprising shall be ;
O the sun and the moon, mother,
Shall both rise with me."

This cherry-tree story occurs in the following scene from one of the Coventry Mystery-Plays, and the carol was probably based upon, or suggested by, it :—

Mary.   Ah, my sweet husband, will ye tell to me, what tree is yon standing upon yon hill ?

Joseph. Forsooth, Mary, it is yclept a cherry-tree, in time of year ye might feed thereon your fill.

Mary.   Turn again, husband, and behold yon tree, now that it bloometh now so sweetly.

Joseph. Come on, Mary, that we were at yon citie or
   else we may be blamed, I tell you lightlie.

Mary. Now, my spouse, I pray you to behold how the
   cherries grow upon yon tree ; for to have
   thereof right fain I would, an it pleased you
   to labour so much for me.

Joseph. Your desire to fulfil I shall assay sickerly,
   Ow, to pluck you of these cherries it is a work
    wild,
   For the tree is so high it will not be lightlie ;
   Therefore let him pluck you cherries, that
    got you with child.

Mary. Now, good Lord, I pray thee, grant me this boon,
   To have of these cherries, if it be your will.
   Now I thank it God, this tree boweth to me
    down.
   I may now gather enow and eat my fill.

Joseph. Ow, I know well I have offended my God in
   Trinity,
   Speaking to my spouse these unkind words ;
   For now I believe my spouse beareth the King's
    Son of bliss.

In the Ille-et-Viliane Department of France there is
a similar fruit-tree legend, but in this case it is told of
an apple tree. Mary is described as longing for the
apples, but Joseph refuses to gather them for her, whereupon the tree bows down of its own accord to Mary and
she plucks off the fruit. Then comes a very interesting

addition to the story, for it relates that Joseph tries to
get some for himself, but, to his great surprise, the
branch springs back out of his reach. Immediately
Joseph perceives this he knows that he has done wrong,
and, falling on his knees, begs for Mary's forgiveness.

This legend of the Cherries is one of the oldest legends
in the world. The Rev. Baring-Gould, the great
authority and writer on Folk-Lore, says :—" The Legend
of the Cherry-Tree is the lingering on of a very curious,
mysterious tradition, common to the whole race of man,
that the eating of the fruit in Eden was the cause of the
descendant of Eve becoming the mother of Him who
was to wipe away that old transgression. In the Carol
and the Mystery-Play this tradition is strangely altered,
but its presence cannot fail to be detected. The
following is from the last Runa or Canto of the " Kale-
wala," the great Finnish Epic, dating from a remote
antiquity :—

" Mariatta, the beautiful maiden, grew up in the
lofty mansion ; the log of the threshold was stroked by
her soft garments, the door-posts by the waving locks
of her head.

" Mariatta, the beautiful maiden, always innocent
and always pure, went forth to milk the cows.

" Mariatta, the beautiful maiden, always innocent
and always pure, went forth to pasture sheep.

" She led them where the serpent glides under the
bushes, and where the lizard darts.

" But no serpent glided, no lizard darted, where Mariatta led her sheep.

" On a hill grew a little berry-tree, and it had a green branch, and on the green branch grew a scarlet berry.

" ' Come, O Virgin ! ' said the tree, ' Come and gather me.'

" ' O Virgin with the tin brooch, come before the worm wounds me, and the black snake has coiled round me.'

" Mariatta, the beautiful maiden, comes forward to pluck the berry, but she cannot reach it. Then she takes a stick and strikes it off, and the berry falls on the ground.

" ' Little berry, scarlet berry, come upon my lap.' And the berry danced upon her lap.

" ' Little berry, scarlet berry, come up to my lips.' And the berry leapt into her mouth, and she swallowed it."

Mariatta becomes the mother of Ilmori (the Air), and when he is born the old Wäinämoinen, the national god of the Finns, " sang his last song, and made a boat of brass, a boat with keep of iron, and in this boat he rowed away, far away into the vast spaces, to the lower regions of the sky." *

Apart from its value as a piece of the literature of antiquity, which shows how this old legend of the

*Introduction to Chope's Carols.

berries has come right down through the centuries to survive as a simple carol, it is also interesting to see how prophetic a picture is the old Finnish Myth of Christianity conquering Paganism, and of the old heathen gods of Mythology flying away and vanishing into the cold and darkness of the bitter north, before the rising warmth and radiance of the coming Christ-child.

Go down go down to yonder town
And sit in the gallery,
And there you'll see sweet Jesus Christ,
Nailed to a big yew-tree.

The following traditional carol of "The Seven Virgins" is of an entirely different type. It is not really a Christmas carol, but is allied in character to the Mystery-Plays. It is, however, so quaint and curious, and so naturally a carol of the people, that it is introduced here as a specimen of interest.

All under the leaves, and the leaves of life,
    I met with virgins seven,
And one of them was Mary mild,
    Our Lord's mother of heaven.

"O what are you seeking, you seven fair maids,
    All under the leaves of life;
Come tell, come tell, what seek you,
    All under the leaves of life?"

"We're seeking for no leaves, Thomas,
    But for a friend of thine,
We're seeking for sweet Jesus Christ,
    To be our guide and thine."

"Go down, go down to yonder town,
    And sit in the gallery,
And there you'll see sweet Jesus Christ
    Nailed to a big yew-tree."

So down they went to yonder town
    As fast as foot could fall,
And many a grievous bitter tear,
    From the Virgin's eye did fall.

" O peace, mother, O peace, mother,
　　Your weeping doth me grieve ;
I must suffer thus," he said,
　" For Adam and for Eve."

" O mother, take you John Evangelist
　　All for to be your son,
And he will comfort you sometimes,
　　Mother, as I have done."

" O come thou, John Evangelist,
　　Thou'rt welcome unto me,
But more welcome my own dear Son
　　Whom I nursed on my knee."

Then he laid his head on his right shoulder,
　　Seeing death it struck him nigh,
" The holy Mother be with your soul,
　　I die, mother, I die."

O the rose, the gentle rose,
　　And the fennel that grows so green,
God give us grace in every place
　　To pray for our King and Queen.

Furthermore for our enemies all
　　Our prayers they should be strong :
Amen, good Lord ; your charity
　　Is the ending of my song.

Another of these interesting legendary carols is the Carol of St. Stephen, which is founded upon the old story that Stephen was " clerk " to King Herod at Jerusalem at the time the Star of Bethlehem appeared. It begins thus :—

> St. Stephen was a clerk,
> In King Herod's hall,
> And served him of bread and cloth
> As ever King befall.

> Stephen out of kitchen came
> With boar's head in hand.
> He saw a star was fair and bright
> Over Bethlehem stand.

The poem goes on to relate that when Stephen saw the Star he became so fearfully excited that, throwing down the boar's head, he rushed into the hall, calling out to King Herod :—

> I forsake thee, Herod,
> And thy werkès all.
> There is a child in Beth'lem born,
> Is better than we all.

Herod, astonished at the extraordinary behaviour of Stephen, demanded "What ailed him ? Did he lack meat or clothes, or was he mad ? "   But Stephen, still excited at the sight of the Star, cried out :—

> " There is a child in Bethlehem born,
> Shall helpen us at our need."

Then Herod, becoming angry, tells Stephen that such an event is as likely to happen as that the capon lying on the dish before him would crow, whereupon, so the legend says, the capon rose up in the dish and crew: " Christus natus est," among the Lordes all, at which Herod and his men became furious, threw out Stephen and stoned him, and the carol ends :—

<blockquote>
And therefore is his even

On Christes owne day,
</blockquote>

alluding to the fact that St. Stephen's Day being the next day after Christmas Day, Christmas Day thus becomes the " Eve " of St. Stephen. Another version of the same legend is given by Vincent de Beauvais, in which two men are seated at dinner. The one who is carving the fowl tells the other that he will cut it up so thoroughly that not even the Lord Himself could make it whole again. No sooner had he spoken the words than the cock stood up with all its feathers on and crowed, and both the men were instantly smitten with leprosy.

THE BOAR'S HEAD CAROL.

The Boar's Head Carol which is sung every Christmas at Queen's College, Oxford, when the boar's head is brought in on a charger is also a traditional carol of the narrative class. The story connected with this quaint custom is that a student of Queen's was walking in the country, near Shotover, a hill near Oxford, studying his Aristotle, when a wild boar rushed suddenly out of

the forest and attacked him. The student being taken
unawares, and not quite knowing what else to do,
crammed the volume down the throat of the beast, and
thus saved his life. Ever since, tradition says, the
boar's head has been served up at dinner at Queen's
College every Christmas, and the carol sung to com-
memorate the student's fortunate escape.

The Precentor, or some other appointed soloist, sings
the chant, and the students join in the refrain, "*Caput
apri defero*," etc.

THE BOAR'S HEAD CAROL.

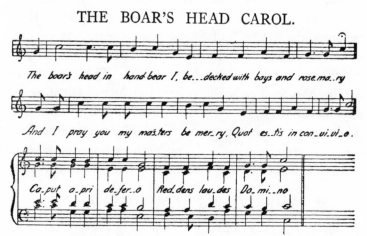

The boar's head in hand bear I, be...decked with bays and rose ma..ry

And I pray you my masters be mer..ry, Quot es..tis in con..vi..vi..o.

Caput a..pri de..fer..o Red..dens lau..des Do..mi...no

The Boar's head, as I understand,
Is the finest dish in all the land,
Which thus bedecked with a gay garland,
Let us *servire cantico.*
    Caput apri defero,
    Reddens laudes Domino.

Our steward hath provided this
In honour of the king of bliss ;
That on this day to be served is,
In reginensis atrio.
   Caput apri defero,
   Reddens laudes Domino.

In comparison with the above it will be interesting
to read the original version as given in the collection of
Wynkyn de Worde, and printed on a single leaf, all that
remains of his book of " Christmasse Carolles " printed
in 1521. The " Bore's Head " carol thus has the dis-
tinction of being the earliest known specimen of the
printed carol, having been printed forty-seven years
after Caxton introduced printing into England.

A CAROL BRYNGING IN THE BORE'S HEED.
  The bore's heed in hand bring I,
  With garlans gay and rosemary,
  I pray you all sing merely
     Qui estis in convivio.

  The bore's heed, I understande,
  Is the chefe servyce in this lande,
  Loke where ever it be fande,
     Servite cum cantico.

  Be gladde lordes, both more and lasse,
  For this hath ordeyned our stewarde,
  To chere you all this Christemasse,
     The Bore's heed with mustarde.

A carol which must have been very popular at one
time, judging from the many variants which still exist,
is the quaint specimen, " I saw three ships come sailing
in." Hone calls it " Christmas Day in the morning."
Ritson, in his " Introduction to Scottish Songs," gives
a version which ends as follows :—

> There comes a ship far sailing then,
> Saint Michael was the stieres-man ;
> Saint John sate in the horn :
> Our Lord harpéd, our Ladye sang,
> And all the bells of heaven they rang
> On Christes Sunday at morn.

Another popular version began :—

> As I sat on a sunny bank,
> A sunny bank, a sunny bank,
> As I sat on a sunny bank
> On Christmas Day in the morning,

and ends with this curious stanza about Joseph and his
" fayre ladye " in the ship :—

> O ! he did whistle and she did sing,
> And all the bells on earth did ring,
> For joy that our Saviour he was born,
> On Christmas Day in the morning.

Here is the complete version, which is probably of fifteenth-century origin :—

I saw three ships come sailing in,
On Christmas Day, on Christmas Day ;
I saw three ships come sailing in
On Christmas day in the morning.

And who was in those ships all three,
On Christmas Day, on Christmas Day ?
And who was in those ships all three
On Christmas Day in the morning ?

Our Saviour Christ and his Ladye,
On Christmas Day, on Christmas Day ;
Our Saviour Christ and his Ladye,
On Christmas Day in the morning.

Pray whither sailed those ships all three,
On Christmas Day, on Christmas Day ?
Pray whither sailed those ships all three,
On Christmas Day in the morning ?

O they sailed into Bethlehem,
On Christmas Day, on Christmas Day ;
O they sailed into Bethlehem,
On Christmas Day in the morning.

And who was in those ships all three,
Our Saviour Christ & his Ladye.

And all the bells on earth shall ring,
On Christmas Day, on Christmas Day,
And all the bells on earth shall ring,
On Christmas Day in the morning.

And all the angels in Heaven shall sing,
On Christmas Day, on Christmas Day ;
And all the angels in Heaven shall sing,
On Christmas Day in the morning.

And all the souls on earth shall sing,
On Christmas Day, on Christmas Day ;
And all the souls on earth shall sing,
On Christmas Day in the morning.

Then let us all rejoice amain,
On Christmas Day, on Christmas Day ;
Then let us all rejoice amain,
On Christmas Day in the morning.

Some of these old carols were not wanting in a certain sense of humour. The old " Dives and Lazarus " carol, for instance, is one which seems to appeal more strongly to the sense of the ludicrous than to the serious. The words are from an old " Broadside " printed in the eighteenth century, and published by T. Bloomer, Edgbaston Street, Birmingham, and now preserved in the Bodleian Library, Oxford. It is founded on the well-known Gospel Parable, and, according to the carol, Dives was in for a very bad time. It begins :—

> As it fell out upon a day,
> Rich Dives made a feast,
> And he invited all his friends,
> And gentry of the best !

While the feast is proceeding, poor Lazarus comes along
and lies down at Dives' door and asks for food and
drink for the poor, which rich Dives refuses, with
threats, and in the next verse :—

> Dives sent out his merry men,
> To whip poor Lazarus away,
> They had no power to strike a stroke,
> But flung their whips away.

> Then Dives sent out his hungry dogs,
> To bite him as he lay,
> They had no power to bite at all,
> But licked his sores away.

> As it fell out upon a day,
> Poor Lazarus sickened and died ;
> There came two angels out of heaven,
> His soul therein to guide.

> Rise up, rise up, Brother Lazarus,
> And come along with me,
> There's a place in heaven provided for thee,
> To sit upon an angel's knee.*

*The idea of Lazarus "sitting on an angel's knee" was probably
suggested to the writer of the carol by old pictures of Lazarus in
Abraham's bosom.

That, according to the carol, was the end of Lazarus ;
now see what befell the rich and mean Dives :—

> As it fell out upon a day,
> Rich Dives sickened and died,
> There came two serpents out of hell.
> His soul therein to guide.
>
> Rise up, rise up, brother Dives,
> And come along with me,
> For you've a place provided in hell,
> To sit upon a serpent's knee !

Fancy sitting upon a serpent's knee !   Notice also how
the serpents of hell call Dives their brother ! One can
quite well imagine this carol being sung by wandering
Christmas minstrels as a very broad hint to the rich
not to be " stingy " to their poorer brethren.

CAROLS OF NATURE

We are told that when God created the world He made a garden and placed man therein to dress and keep it well, and it was only the disobedience of Adam which drove him forth from that garden of innocence. But the beauty of nature remained, and it is only natural that poets should associate the beauty, purity, and innocence of God's creation with the perfection of the Christ-child, born to redeem the world. Accordingly we find carols written on the subject of birds, flowers, and trees, which connect Man and Nature together as benefiting under the blessings of the Incarnation. For instance, there is a charming old Bas-Quercy Carol,* in which the birds are supposed to have come to Bethlehem to rejoice at the birth of the Saviour, and each bird sings its own song in its own way to the little one. Then, again, in the Carol of the Flowers, another Bas-Quercy carol, the flowers are called to pay their adoration to the Saviour, the blossoms being made to typify the virtues of Christ. Although the melody is written in a major mode and sounds rather modern, it is really

*See Soleville's Chants populaires du Bas-Quercy.

old, being founded upon another version of the same tune which was in use in the seventeenth century.

THE CAROL OF THE FLOWERS. (NOUEL DE LAS FLOUS.)

Sweet-est flowers O come and in a beau-teous ring, Spread your love-ly
Fine

per-fumes round your heaven-ly King. Ti--ny Vio-let, emblem of all mod-es-
repeat D.C.

-ty, show how humble He is made for you and me;

Verse 2.   Lovely Lily, emblem of all purity,
        He is born of Mary, who is pure as thee.
                    Sweetest flowers, etc.

     3.   Little Pansy, glowing all with colour bright,
        See He glows more lovely with a heavenly
        light.
                    Sweetest flowers, etc.

     4.   Sweetest Rose, thou emblem of eternal love,
        Thus He draws us all with Him to heaven
        above.
          Sweetest flowers, O come, and in a beau-
          teous ring, etc.

Hone, in his book of " Ancient Mysteries," gives the following account of a curious old printed broad-sheet.

At the top is a heading, " Christus natus est " (Christ is born), and a wood-cut, 10 inches high, 8½ inches wide, representing the stable at Bethlehem. The Christ-child lies in the crib, watched by the Virgin and Joseph, and kneeling shepherds and attending angels. There is a man playing on the bagpipes and a woman with a basket of fruit on her head. The rest of the figures are : a sheep bleating, an ox lowing, a raven croaking, a crow cawing on the hayrack, a cock crowing up above, and the angels singing in the sky. The animals have labels from their mouths bearing Latin inscriptions. Down the side of the woodcut is the following account and explanation :—A religious man invented the conceits of both birds and beasts, drawn in the picture of our Saviour's birth doth thus express them :—

The Cock croweth, *Christus natus est,* Christ is born.
The Raven asked, *Quando ?*　　When ?
The Cow replied, *Hac nocte,*　　This night.
The Ox crieth out, *Ubi, Ubi ?*　　Where ? Where ?
The Sheep bleateth out, *Bethlehem,*　Bethlehem.
Voice from heaven soundeth, *Gloria in excelsis,*
　　　　　　　Glory be on high.

TREES

In our own country the Holly and Ivy hold the chief place among the Nature carols. The use of these plants in the decoration of churches and homes at Christmastide has probably come down to us from some ancient form of Nature worship. Tree-worship has been found in every land and amongst every race of mankind. The Scandinavians, for instance, imagined a great tree of life with its roots in the centre of the earth. Again, the Druids looked upon the oak as a peculiarly sacred tree embodying a spirit, which, when the oak died down in the winter, left the oak tree and went to live in the mistletoe which grew on it, and at their Winter-feast time they ceremoniously cut the mistletoe from the oak with a golden sickle, caught it in a white sheet, and deposited it on their altars at their sacrifices. Christianity, too, has many stories and legends connected with trees, from the famous tree in the Garden of Eden downwards. In fact, tree stories are endless. From an examination of the old carols it appears that the two characteristic English plants of the season, the holly and the ivy, seemed to have been looked upon as representing the two sexes, the holly the young men, and the ivy the maidens, and many poems take the form of an argument between them, as is shown by the following fifteenth-century carol :—

> Holly and Ivy made a great party,
> Who should have the mastery
>   In landes where they go.
>
> Then spake Holly, " I am free and jolly,
> I will have the mastery,
>   In landes where we go."
>
> Then spake Ivy, " I am loved and proud,
> And I will have the mastery,
>   In landes where we go."
>
> Then spake Holly, and set him on his knee,
> " I pray thee, gentle Ivy,
> Say me no villainy
>   In landes where we go."

With reference to this rivalry of the sexes as represented by the Holly and Ivy, there is an amusing story related in Pasquil's " Jests," 1609, and told again in Sandy's " Christmas Carols," of an old knight, who, " being disposed to make himself merry at Christmastide, sent for his tenants, together with their wives, to dine with him in the great hall. When meat had been set upon the table he commanded that no man should

drink until he that was master over his wife should
sing a carol, to excuse all the company. Great niceness
there was who should be the musician now the cuckoo-
time was so far off. Yet with much ado, looking one
upon another, after a dry ahem or two, a dreaming
companion drew out as much as he durst towards an
ill-fashioned ditty. When, having made an end, to the
great comfort of his beholders, at last it came to the
women's table, where likewise commandment was given
that there should no drink be touched till she that was
master over her husband had sung a Christmas carol,
whereupon they fell all to such a singing that there was
never heard such a caterwauling piece of music, whereat
the knight laughed heartily, that it did him half as
much good as a corner of his Christmas pie."

The following carol is to be found in the Harley MSS.
in the British Museum. It dates from the time of
Henry VI., and seems to convey the same sentiments
as the preceding example :—

Nay, Ivy, nay, it shall not be I wis ;
Let Holly have the mastery, as the manner is.
Holly standeth in the hall, fair to behold ;
Ivy stands without the door, she is full sore a-cold.
　　　Nay, Ivy, Nay, etc.

Holly and his merry men they dauncen and they sing,
Ivy and her maidens they weepen and they wring.
　　　Nay, Ivy, Nay, etc.

Ivy hath a kybe,* she caught it with the cold,
So may they all have that do with Ivy hold.
      Nay, Ivy, Nay, etc.

Holly he hath berries as red as any rose,
The forester, the hunters keep (them) from the does.
      Nay, Ivy, Nay, etc.

Ivy she hath berries as black as any sloes,
There comes the owl and eats them as she goes.
      Nay, Ivy, Nay, etc.

Holly he hath birdes a fair full flock,
The nightingale, the popinjay, the gentle laverock.
      Nay, Ivy, Nay, etc.

Good Ivy, what birdes hast thou ?
None but the owlet that cries " How, How."
      Nay, Ivy, Nay, etc.

The Holly and Ivy carols of a religious type are few.
In the following traditional carol, which was printed in
a " broadside " at the beginning of the eighteenth century, the holly and its berries, etc., are made typical of
St. Mary and the Holy Child. Notice the curious
blending of nature and religion in the refrain, " O the
rising of the sun," which follows each stanza.

* Kybe = chilblain.

The holly bears a blossom
As whitest lily flower ;
And Mary bore sweet Jesus Christ
To be our sweet Saviour.
   O the rising of the sun, etc.

The holly bears a berry,
As red as any blood ;
And Mary bore sweet Jesus Christ
To do poor sinners good.
   O the rising of the sun, etc.

The holly bears a prickle
As sharp as any thorn ;
And Mary bore sweet Jesus Christ
On Christmas Day in the morn.
  O the rising of the sun, etc.

The holly bears a bark,
As bitter as any gall ;
And Mary bore sweet Jesus Christ
For to redeem us all.
  O the rising of the sun, etc.

The holly and the ivy
Are both now fully grown ;
Of all the trees that are in the wood
The holly bears the crown.
  O the rising of the sun, etc.

The holly was formerly affectionately called in Cornwall Aunt Mary's Tree, and the following excellent modern carol written in the old style by Robert Stephen Hawker, the famous Vicar of Morwenstowe, perpetuates the name :—

MODRYB MARYA—AUNT MARY.

Now of all the trees by the King's highway,
  Which do you love the best ?
O ! the bush that is green upon Christmas Day,
  The bush with the bleeding breast.
Now the holly with her drops of blood for me :
For that is our dear Aunt Mary's Tree.

The leaves are sweet with our Saviour's name,
  'Tis a plant that loves the poor ;
Summer and winter it shines the same,
  Beside the cottage door.
O ! the holly with her drops of blood for me :
For that is our kind Aunt Mary's Tree.

'Tis a bush that the birds will never leave ;
  They sing in it all day long ;
But sweetest of all upon Christmas Eve,
  Is to hear the robin's song.
'Tis the merriest sound upon earth and sea :
For it comes from our own Aunt Mary's Tree.

So of all that grow by the King's highway,
  I love that tree the best ;
'Tis a bower for the birds upon Christmas Day,
  The bush of the bleeding breast.
O ! the holly with her drops of blood for me :
For that is our sweet Aunt Mary's Tree.

SPRING CAROLS

Through all the manifestations of the spirit of nature, whether in her wildest or most peaceful moments, a perfect harmony prevails, and man, as much a child of nature as are the birds and beasts, naturally reflects her moods in his music. In the spring the whole of nature revives from her winter rest; the birds, flowers, and beasts respond to that unwritten law which calls them to renewed life and energy; what wonder then if man himself, feeling the marvellous stir of spring, breaks forth into a song of joy and happiness? In the "Piae Cantiones," printed in Sweden in 1582, is an interesting Latin specimen of an old Spring Song, "Tempus adest floridum," with an excellent tune which Dr. Neale adapted to his own words, "Good King Wenceslas," and choirs and congregations little imagine when they sing this carol at Christmas-tide that they are singing an old melody written for the following spring-song and probably composed in the thirteenth century.

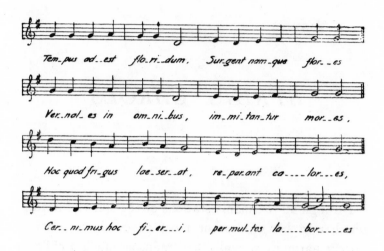

Prata plena floribus jucunda aspectu,
Ubi juvat cernere herbas cum delectu
Gramina et plantae quae hyeme quiescunt,
Vernali in tempore vivunt et accrescunt.

Haec vobis pulcre monstrant Deum Creatorem,
Quem quoque nos credimus omnium factorem :
Tempus ergo hilare, quo laetari libet,
Renovato nam mundo, nos novari decet.

Res ornatur floribus et multo decore,
Nos honestis moribus et vero amore,
Gaudeamus igitur tempore jucundo,
Laudemusque Dominum pectoris ex fundo.

When a poor man came in sight✛
Gath'ring winter fuel✛✛✛✛✛✛✛

Another spring carol from the same book is "In vernali tempore," a verse of which is given below. The melody of this also was used by Dr. Neale for an Epiphany carol, "O'er the hill and o'er the dale come three kings together." •

Here is the first verse of Dr. Neale's words, which, although excellent in themselves, have nothing whatever to do with the original :—

> O'er the hill and o'er the dale
> Come three kings together,
> Caring nought for snow and hail,
> Wind and storm and weather.
> Now on Persia's sandy plain,
> Now where Tigris swells with rain,
> They their camels tether.

This is the original version :—

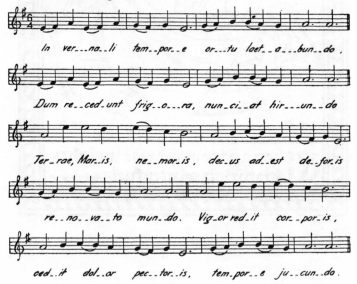

In ver...na..li tem..por..e   or...tu laet...a...bun..do ,

Dum re..ced.unt frig..o...ra, nun..ci..at hir...un..do

Ter..rae, Mar..is,   ne..mor..is , dec..us ad..est de..for.is

re..no..va..to mun..do.   Vig..or red..it cor..por..is ,

ced..it dol..or pec..tor..is , tem..por..e ju..cun..do .

In the Harleian Collection, in the British Museum, is preserved an old English carol of spring-time of the thirteenth century, " Sumer is i-cumen in," which is famous as the earliest known specimen of the musical form of the Rota, or Round. It is supposed to have been written at the Abbey of Reading by a monk named John of Fornsete, about the year 1226. It is a " round " for four equal voices, with a drone-bass in two parts underneath, and is a perfect specimen of a complete musical composition, and in fact is the earliest known example extant that can be really called a musical composition. The melody is bright and flowing, and the harmonic effect as the " parts " of the round come in in their order is quite satisfactory to modern ears. Only one or two words need a little change to modernise the song also

LULLABIES
AND CRADLE SONGS

Nothing appeals more strongly to the whole human race than the simple, peaceful, and homely picture of a mother lulling her little child to rest and crooning over it her " baby-songs " as she rocks it to sleep. Such a picture of pure love and happiness has stirred the best emotions in the poets, musicians, and painters of all times, and it is only natural that many beautiful carols should have been written around the subject of the Virgin and Child, and there is a large collection of these little outpourings on the human side of Christianity. They seem to have been either suggested by the crèches set up in churches, or were written for the Mystery-Plays. Many of the old mediæval ones are in Latin A well-known and charming specimen begins :—

> Dormi, fili dormi, mater
> Cantat unigenito ;
> Dormi puer, dormi, pater
> Nato clamat parvulo.
> Mille tibi laudes canimus,
> Mille, Millie, Millies.

which may be roughly translated :—

> Sleep, baby, sleep, the mother
> Sings to the only-begotten one ;
> Sleep, baby, sleep, the father
> Calls to the new-born little one.
> Thousand songs to Thee we sing,
> Thousand, thousand, thousands.

Our own English writers produced some of the most beautiful of the Lullaby carols. Amongst the oldest, both as to the music and words, is a little fifteenth-century one, to be found in the British Museum in a small volume written by Friar John Brackley, of Norwich, in the reign of Richard II. There are several other carols in the same book by the same author.

> I saw a sweet and seemly sight,
> A blissful maid, a blossom bright,
> That moaning made and mirth of mange,*
> A maiden mother meek and mild,
> In cradle keep a knave† child
> That softly slept, she sat and sang,
> > Lullay, Lully, Lullay.

The following simple and beautiful old English Lullaby, well known as the Coventry carol, is from the sixteenth century Coventry Corpus Christi play, entitled " The Pageant of the Shearmen and Tailors," and simply

---

* of mange=of manger ?
† knave=boy.

breathes love for " the poor youngling." The melody to which it is set is equally charming. Although written in a minor mode, it ends with the major third of the scale, which has a most beautiful effect when sung, unaccompanied, by a choir of trained singers.

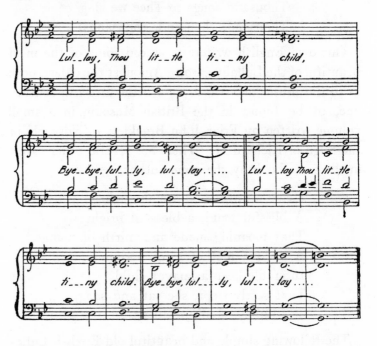

Many of the Cradle Songs take the form of an imaginary duologue between the mother and child, as in this lovely old English one of the fifteenth century, which is to be found at the British Museum in Royal Appendix 58, fol. 52. The stanzas are spoken alternately by Mother and Child, each ending with the refrain, " Bye-bye, lullay." The music of the refrain is written in three parts, with the melody in the middle. The tune of the solo verses is very similar to the melody of the refrain, with slight variations to fit the words. (A simple harmony is added by the writer.)

There are several versions of this old carol. In the present version some words have been modernised, but the original is fairly closely followed.

This endernight
I saw a sight,
A star as bright as day ;
And listened long*
A maiden's song,
" *Bye-bye, lully, lullay.*"

The lovely lady sat and sang†
And to her Child did say :
My Son, my lord, my darling dear,
Why liest thou in hay,
Mine own dear son,
Whence are Thou come ?
Art Thou not God alway ?
But none the less
I will not cease
To sing *Bye-bye, lullay.*

Then spake the Child that was so young,
And thus methought He said :
Yea I am known as heaven's King,
Though now in crib am laid,
But angels bright round Me shall light,
And guard me night and day,
And in that sight thou mayest delight
And sing *Bye-bye, lullay.*

*Original : " And ever among."
†Dr. W. H. Frere gives :
          " This Virgin dear,
            Withouten fear
            Unto her Son gan say :
            My Son, my Lord,
            My Father dear."

Now my sweet son, the heaven's own King,
Why art Thou laid in stall ?
Why hast Thou no rich bedding spread
In some great kinge's hall ?
Methinks of right the Lord of might
Should lie in rich array :
But nevertheless I will not cease
To sing *Bye-bye, lullay.*

O Mary Mother, Queen of bliss,
Though I be laid in stall,
The lords and dukes and kings so great
Shall come and worship all.
And ye shall see
That wise kings three
Shall come on the twelfth day ;
For this behest
Give me thy breast,
And sing *Bye-bye, lullay.*

Now tell me sweet, my darling son,
That art to me so dear,
How should I keep thee every day
And make thee glad of cheer ?
For all Thy will
I would fulfil,
Thou knowest it well, in fay ;
I will thee kiss
And make Thee bliss,
And sing *Bye-bye, lullay.*

O Lovely Lady, Mother dear,
Take thou Me up aloft,
And set Me down upon thy knee,
And dangle Me full oft,
Within thine arms.
Thou'lt keep me warm,
And guard Me night and day ;
And if I weep
And do not sleep,
Then sing *Bye-bye, lullay.*

Now my sweet son, since it is so,
All things are at Thy will,
Grant me, I pray
This boon to-day,
If it be right and skill,*
That all who can,
Or child, or man,
Be merry on this day :
To bliss them bring,
And I shall sing
Lullay, Bye-bye, lullay.

Another interesting lullaby carol is the following,
taken from William Byrd's " Psalms, Sonets, and Songs
of Sadnes and Pietie," and published in London in 1588.
Herod's massacre of the innocents is a very common
subject in these children's carols. Notice how the refrain, " O woe and woeful heavy day " changes to
" O joy and joyful happy day " in the last stanza.

*Skill = fitting.

Lulla, la lulla, lulla, lullaby.
My sweet little baby, what meanest Thou to cry?
Be still, my blessed babe, though cause Thou hast to
    mourn,
Whose blood most innocent the cruel king has sworn,
And lo, alas ! behold what slaughter he doth make,
Shedding the blood of infants all, sweet Saviour, for
    Thy sake.
A heavenly King is born, they say, which King this
    king would kill,
    O woe and woeful heavy day when wretches have their will.

Lulla, la lulla, lulla, lullaby.
My sweet little baby, what meanest Thou to cry?
Three kings this King of kings to see are come from afar.
To each unknown, with offerings (great), by guiding of
    a star ;
And shepherds heard the song which angels bright did
    sing,
Giving all glory unto God for coming of this King,
Which must be made away, King Herod would Him kill.
    O woe and woeful heavy day when wretches have their will.

Lulla, la lulla, lulla, lullaby.
My sweet little baby, what meanest thou to cry?
Lo, my sweet little babe, be still, lament no more :
From fury shalt Thou step aside, help have we still in
    store ;
We heavenly warning have some other soil to seek,
From death must fly the Lord of life, as lamb both mild
    and meek.

Thus must my babe obey the king that would Him kill.
O woe and woeful heavy day when wretches have their will.

Lulla, la lulla, lulla lullaby.
My sweet little baby, what meanest Thou to cry?
But Thou shalt live and reign, as sybils have foresaid,
And perfect virgin pure, with her breasts shall upbreed
Both God and man that all hath made, the Son of
          heavenly seed,
Whom caitiffs none can 'tray, whom tyrants none can
          kill.
O joy and joyful happy day when wretches want their will.

The whole piece, a " serious " madrigal in five parts,
by William Byrd (Br. Museum K 2, f. 1) is remarkably
fine, musically. The refrain " Lulla, la lulla," etc., is
printed by itself as No. 497 of Novello's " Musical
Times," and is as charming a lullaby as can be imagined.
It is purposely much less grave in character than the
remainder of the composition, and may be sung without
difficulty by two Sopranos, Alto, Tenor and Bass. It will
richly repay the pains spent upon it.

Subjoined is the Title-page of Byrd's work.

Superius

Psalmes, Sonets and Songs of Sadnes and pietie made
into Musicke of fiue parts : whereof some of them going
abroade among diuers, in untrue coppies are heere
truely corrected, and th'other being Songs very rare
and newly composed are heere published for the

recreation of all such as delight in Musicke : By William Byrd,

> one of the Gent. of the Queenes Maiesties
> honorable Chappell

[vignette]

Printed by Thomas East, the assigne of W. Byrd, and are to be sold at the dwelling house of the said T. East,

> by Paules wharfe
> 1588
> *Cum privilegio Regiæ Maiestatis*

At the back of the title-page is the following :—
Reasons briefely set downe by th'auctor to perswade every one to learne to sing.

First, it is a knowledge easely taught, anu quickly learned, where there is a good Master and an apt Scoller.

2. The exercise of singing is delightfull to Nature and good to preserue the health of Man.

3. It doth strengthen all parts of the brest, and doth open the pipes.

4. It is a singular good remedie for a stutting and stamering in the speech.

5. It is the best meanes to procure a perfect pronunciation & to make a good Orator.

6. It is the onely way to know where Nature hath bestowed the benefit of a good voyce : which guift is so rare, as there is not one among a thousand, that hath it : & in many that excellent guift is lost, because they want Art to expresse Nature.

7. There is not any Musicke of Instruments whatsoeuer, comparable to that which is made of the voyces of Men, where the voyces are good, and the same well sorted and ordered.

8. The better the voyce is, the meeter it is to honour and serue God therewith ; and the voyce of Man is chiefly to be imployed to that ende.
   Omnis Spiritus laudet Dominum
   Since singing is so good a thing
   I wish all men would learne to sing.

Dedicated (on next page) to the Right Honorable Sir Christopher Halton, Kt., Lord Chancellor of England.

THE CHILDHOOD
OF CHRIST

In an old manuscript in the British Museum there
are many traditional stories of the life of Christ, amongst
them being the legend of the Holy Well. This story,
like the story of the " Carnal and the Crane," and
others, has come down to us in the shape of a traditional
carol, and probably dates from the fifteenth century.
Perhaps it is the best known and most interesting of all
the carols on the boyhood of Christ.

Little Jesus, like all children, loved to be with play-
mates, and one day obtained permission from his mother
to play with other children down by the Holy Well.
These youngsters proved to be " lords' and ladies' sons,"
and knowing how poor and lowly were Jesus' parents,
they objected to him, and twitted him with his mean
birth. This unkindness hurt the feelings of the tender
Christ-child, who poured out his sorrows to his mother.
Mary was naturally indignant at the insult given to her
heavenly boy, and she asked him to exercise his great
powers to punish the other children for their insults.

But the love and mercy of Christ is shown in the child's gentle answer, full of love and pity for the proud children who did not understand :—

> " Nay, nay," sweet Jesus gently said,
> " Nay, nay, that must not be,
> For there are many sinful souls
> Crying out for help from me."

THE HOLY WELL.

> As it fell out one May morning,
>   And on a bright holyday,
> Sweet Jesus asked of his dear mother,
>   If He might go and play.
>
> To play, to play, sweet Jesus shall go,
>   And to play now get you gone,
> And let me hear of no complaint,
>   At night when you come home.
>
> Sweet Jesus went to yonder town,
>   As far as the Holy Well,
> And there did see as fine children
>   As any tongue can tell.
>
> He said, " God bless you every one,
>   May Christ your portion be ;
> Little children, shall I play with you ?
>   And you shall play with me."

THE HOLY WELL.

As it fell out on one May morning,
And upon one bright holiday,
Sweet Jesus asked of his dear Mother
If he might go to play.

To play to play sweet Jesus shall go,
And to play pray get you gone,
And let me hear of no complaint
At night when you come home.

But they made answer to him, " No!"
  They were lords' and ladies' sons ;
And he, the meanest of them all,
  Was born in an ox's stall.

Sweet Jesus turned him around,
  And he neither laughed nor smiled,
But the tears came trickling from his eyes,
  Like water from the skies.

Sweet Jesus turned him about,
  To his mother's dear home went he,
And said, " I have been in yonder town,
  As after you may see.

" I have been down in yonder town,
  As far as the Holy Well ;
There did I meet as fine children
  As any tongue can tell.

" I bid God bless them every one,
  And Christ their bodies see ;
Little children shall I play with you ?
  And you shall play with me.

" But they made answer to me, ' No,'
  They were lords' and ladies' sons ;
And I, the meanest of them all,
  Was born in an ox's stall."

" Though you are but a maiden's child,
    Born in an ox's stall,
Thou are the Christ, the King of heaven,
    And the Saviour of them all.

" Sweet Jesus, go down to yonder town,
    As far as the Holy Well,
And take away those sinful souls,
    And dip them deep in hell."

" Nay, nay," sweet Jesus mildly said,
    " Nay, nay, that must not be,
For there are many sinful souls
    Crying out for the help of me."

The Carnal and the Crane.

This traditional carol, though not so old as the carol of St. Stephen, introduces the same legend of the capon. (See the carol of St. Stephen, page 42). The carol is an imaginary conversation between a carnal (i.e., a crow) and a crane. The poem naturally divides itself into two sections, the first dealing with the Nativity (including the birth of Christ, the coming of the wise men, and the legend of the capon), the second with the flight into Egypt and the legends of the " lovely lion " and the miraculous growth of corn.

As I passed by a river-side,
  And there as I did rein,
In argument I chanced to hear,
  A carnal and a crane.

The carnal said unto the crane,
  " If all the world should turn,
Before we had the Father,
  But now we have the Son,

From whence does the Son come ?
  From where and from what place ? "
He said, " In a manger,
  Between an ox and ass."

" I pray thee," said the carnal,
  " Tell me before thou go,
Was not the mother of Jesus
  Conceived by the Holy Ghost ? "

" She was the purest virgin,
  And pure from every sin ;
She was the handmaid of our Lord,
  And mother of our King."

" Where is the golden cradle
  That Christ was rocked in ?
Where are the silken sheets
  That Jesus was wrapt in ? "

" A manger was the cradle
  That Christ was rocked in,
The provender the asses left,
  So sweetly he slept on.

There was a star in the West land,
  So bright it did appear,
Into King Herod's chamber,
  And where King Herod were.

The Wise Men soon espied it,
  And told the King on high,
A princely babe was born that night,
  No king could e'er destroy."

' If this be true,' King Herod said,
  ' As thou tellest unto me,
This roasted cock that lies in the dish,
  Shall crow full fences three.'

The cock soon freshly feathered was,
  By the work of God's own hand,
And then three fences crowed he,
  In the dish where he did stand.

' Rise up, rise up, you merry men all,
  See that you ready be,
All children under two years old
  Now slain they all shall be.'

Then Jesus, ah! and Joseph,
　　And Mary, that was so pure,
They travelled into Egypt,
　　As you shall find it sure.

And when they came to Egypt's land,
　　Amongst those fierce wild beasts,
Mary, she being weary,
　　Must need sit down to rest.

'Come, sit thee down,' said Jesus,
　　'Come sit thee down by me,
And thou shalt see how those wild beasts
　　Do come and worship me.'

First came the lovely lion,
　　Which Jesus' grace did spring,
And of the wild beasts in the field,
　　The lion shall be the king.

We'll choose our virtuous princes,
　　Of birth and high degree,
In every sundry nation,
　　Wherever we come and see.

Then Jesus, ah! and Joseph,
　　And Mary that was unknown,
Then travelled by a husbandman,
　　Just while his seed was sown.

' God speed thee, man," said Jesus,
  ' Go, fetch thy ox and wain,
And carry home thy corn again,
  Which thou hast this day sown.'

The husbandman fell on his knees,
  Even before his face ;
' Long time hast thou been looked for,
  But now thou art come at last.

And I myself do now believe,
  Thy name is Jesus called ;
Redeemer of mankind thou art,
  Though undeserving all.'

' The truth, man, thou hast spoken,
  Of it thou mayst be sure,
For I must lose my precious blood
  For thee and thousands more.

If any one should come this way,
  And enquire for me alone,
Tell them that Jesus passed by
  Whenas thy seed was sown.

After that there came King Herod,
  With his train so furiously,
Enquiring of the husbandman,
  Whether Jesus passed by.

' Why the truth it must be spoke,
　　And the truth it must be known,
For Jesus passed by this way,
　　Whenas my seed was sown.

But now I have it reapen,
　　And some laid on my wain,
Ready to fetch and carry
　　Into my barn again.'

' Turn back now,' says the Captain,
　　Your labour and mine's in vain,
It's full three-quarters of a year
　　Since he his seed has sown.'

So Herod was deceived
　　By the work of God's own hand,
And further he proceeded
　　Into the Holy Land.

There's thousands of young children,
　　Which for His sake did die ;
Do not forbid these little ones,
　　And do not them deny.

The truth now I have spoken,
　　And the truth now have I shown ;
How the ever blessed Virgin,
　　She brought us forth a Son."

Thus wicked Herod and his men, who had intended to overtake and kill the young child Jesus, were deceived by the sight of the miraculously grown field of corn, which had sprung up at the word of Jesus, immediately after it had been sown !

NUMERAL CAROLS

Another quaint form is the Numeral Carol, in which the numbers are made to rhyme with words. They were very common in the olden time. A well-known specimen is " The Seven Joys of Mary," or the " New Dial," once very popular in the West Country. The " New Dial " evidently derives its title from the figures on the Sun-dial.

The first good joy that Ma.ry had it was the joy of one

To see her dear Son Je.sus Christ when He was first her Son.

When He was first her Son,goodman, And hap.py may we be

Praise Fa.ther, Son and Ho..ly Ghost,through all e..ter..ni....ty

This curious old carol goes through all the numbers up to seven :—

The joy of two rhymes with " making the lame to go."

    ,,   ,,   three   ,,   ,,   making the blind to see.

    ,,   ,,   four   ,,   ,,   reading the Bible o'er.

    ,,   ,,   five   ,,   ,,   raising the dead alive.

It is considerably startling, however, on reading the " joy of six " to find that it rhymes with

> To see her own Son, Jesus Christ,
> Upon the crucifix.

The joy of seven rhymes with " upon the throne of heaven."

The writer well remembers, when we had a particularly hard winter nearly forty years ago, having heard this same carol tune sung round the streets of London by labouring men out of work, who tramped the streets through the snow, with shovels over their shoulders, singing the following doggerel verse, in the hope of receiving pence from the charitably disposed :—

We're got no work to do......, we've got no work to do

We've got no work to do......, We've got no work to do.....

We're all turned out, poor lab'ring men, We've got no work to do....

There is also a less-known Fifteenth-Century Carol on The *Five* Joys of Mary :—

> The first joy, as I you tell,
> With Mary met Saint Gabriel.
> " Hail Mary, I greet thee well,"
> *With Father and Son and Holy Ghost.*

The second joy be in good fay,
Was on Christemasse Day ;
Born he was all of a may,
   With Father and Son and Holy Ghost.

The third joy, withouten strife,
That blissful Birth was full rife.
Was when He rose from death to life,
   With Father and Son and Holy Ghost.

The fourth joy, in good fay,
Was upon Holy Thursday,
He rose to heaven in rich array,
With Father and Son and Holy Ghost.

The fifth joy without dene,*
In heaven he crowned his mother clean,
That was well with the eyes a-seen,
   With Father and Son and Holy Ghost.

The original of this carol is preserved among the Sloane MSS., and is probably as old as the fifteenth century, perhaps older. The first verse is given as a specimen, with its original spelling.

Joyis FYVE.
Ye ferste joye as i zu telle
W^t Mary met seynt Gab'elle,
Heyl Mary i grete ye welle,
   W^t fad^r & sone & holy gost.

*dene = deny or doubt.

Although very poor stuff indeed and not a carol, the following is inserted as shewing the use of the figures in rhyming up to the number twelve. It is entitled " A New Dial " and is from an old Almanack. It may be seventeenth-century work.

A New Dial.

One God, one Baptism, and one Faith,
One Truth there is, the Scripture saith.

Two Testaments (the Old and New)
We do acknowledge to be true.

Three persons are in Trinity,
Which make one God in Unity.

Four sweet Evangelists are there,
Christ's birth, life, death, which do declare.

Five senses (like Five Kings) maintain
In every Man a several reign.

Six days to labour is not wrong,
For God himself did work so long.

Seven Liberal Arts hath God sent down,
With Divine skill Man's Soul to crown.

Eight in Noah's Ark alive were found,
When (in a word) the World lay drowned.

Nine Muses (like the heaven's Nine Spheres)
With sacred Tunes entice our ears.

Ten Statutes God to Moses gave,
Which kept or broke, do spill or save.

Eleven with Christ in Heaven to dwell,
The Twelfth for ever burns in Hell.

Twelve are attending on God's Son,
Twelve make our Creed.   The Dial's done.

Count One the first hour of thy Birth,
The hours that follow lead to earth ;

Count Twelve, thy doleful striking knell,
And then thy Dial shall go well.

THE WASSAILS

The Wassail is one of the oldest known forms of the English carol, and derives its name from the Anglo-Saxon Weshal, be hale or healthy, a toast equivalent to the modern " Good health." The presence of the Feasting Carol is easily understood, if we remember that most of the great Christian festivals were grafted on to the feast days or festivals of the old heathen mythology. Christmas, for instance, coincides with the time when the Druids celebrated their winter feasts, the Romans the Saturnalia, and the Scandinavians the Feast of the Yule. There exists an old Anglo-Norman Carol of the thirteenth century, " Seignors, ore entendez a nus " (" Lordlings, give ear to us "), which, after recounting the joys of Christmas, and calling upon all to keep up the customs of Christmas generosity, ends with the old Saxon " toast " of " Wassail " and " Drink-hail." It is interesting to imagine bands of minstrels wandering from one castle to another of the Norman nobility, discoursing sweet sounds for the gratification of the assembled guests, and certain of a ready welcome on so festive an occasion as the celebration of the Christmas feast. There is an excellent translation of this old

carol by Mr. F. Douce in Brand's "Antiquities." It
has six verses, all about eating and drinking, with the
refrain :—

> Dieu doint a tuz icels joie d'amurs,
> Qui a Danz Noel ferunt honors.
> *May joy come from God above,*
> *To all those who Christmas love*

at the end of each verse. The first and last two verses
(as translated by Mr. Douce) are as follows :—

ANGLO-NORMAN CAROL.

> Lordlings, listen to our lay.
> We have come from far away
> To seek Christmas ;
> In this mansion we are told,
> He his yearly feast doth hold ;
> 'Tis to-day !
> May joy come from God above,
> To all those who Christmas love.
>
> Lordlings, I now tell you true,
> Christmas bringeth unto you
> Only mirth ;
> His house he fills with many a dish
> Of bread and meat and also fish,
> To grace the day.
> May joy come from God above,
> To all those who Christmas love.

To English ale and Gascon wine,
And French, doth Christmas much incline,
    And Anjous too ;
He makes his neighbour freely drink,
So that in sleep his head doth sink
    Often by day.
May joy come from God above
To all those who Christmas love.

Lords, by Christmas and the host
Of this mansion hear my toast—
    Drink it well—
Each must drain his cup of wine,
And I the first will toss off mine ;
    Thus I advise.
Here then I bid you all *Wassail*,
Cursed be he that will not say, *Drinkhail*.
May joy come from God above,
To all those who Christmas love.

A form of the Wassail, more familiar to English
people, is the well-known North-Country traditional
carol :—

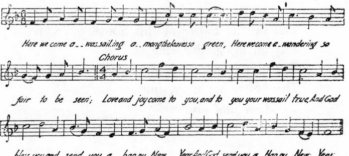

Here we come a-wassailing
Among the leaves so green,
Here we come a-wandering
   So fair to be seen.

     Love and joy come to you,
      And to you your wassail true,
     And God bless you,
      And send you a Happy New Year.

Our Wassail cup is made
Of the Rosemary tree,
And so is your beer
Of the best barley.

     Love and joy, etc.

We are not daily beggars,
That beg from door to door,
But we are neighbour's children,
Whom you have seen before.

     Love and joy, etc.

Call up the butler of this house,
Put on his golden ring,
Bid him bring up a glass of beer,
The better we may sing.
     Love and joy, etc.

We have a little purse,
Made of ratching leather skin,
Give us some of your money,
To line it well within.
    Love and joy, etc.

Bring us out a table,
And spread it with a cloth,
Bring us out a mouldy cheese,
And some of your Christmas-loaf.
    Love and joy, etc.

God bless the master of this house,
Likewise the mistress too.
And all the little children,
That round the table go.
    Love and joy, etc.

Good master and good mistress,
As you sit by the fire,
Pray think of us poor children,
A-wandering in the mire.
    Love and joy, etc.

Another version of this old carol gives us the following :—
    " Here we come *a-whistling*,
    All through the fields so green ;
    Here we come a-singing,
    So fair to be seen," etc.

While the second stanza runs thus :—

> " The roads are very dirty,
> My boots are very thin,
> I have a little pocket
> To put a penny in,"

Which seems to show that the good folk of this period kept up a very effective " St. Boxing Day " without the help of any Bank Holiday Act !

Another of these traditional Wassailers' carols has some amusing references to the horse, mare, and cow of the master.   Dobbin is, of course, the horse, Smiler is the mare, and Fillpail is the cow.

> Wassail, wassail, all over the town,
> Our bread it is white, and our ale it is brown ;
> Our bowl it is made of a maplin tree,
> So here, my good fellow, I'll drink to thee.
>
> The wassailing bowl, with a toast within,
> Come, fill it up, unto the brim ;
> Come, fill it up, that we all may see ;
> With the wassailing bowl I'll drink to thee.
>
> Here's to Dobbin, and to his right ear,
> God send our master a happy New Year ;
> A happy New Year as e'er he did see—
> With the wassailing bowl I'll drink to thee.

HERE·WE·COME·A·WHISTLING·THRO·THE·FIELDS·SO·GREEN·

HERE·WE·COME·A·SINGING·SO·FAIR·TO·BE·SEEN·

HERE·WE·COME·A·WHISTLING·THRO·THE·FIELDS·SO·GREEN
HERE·WE·COME·A·SINGING·SO·FAIR·TO·BE·SEEN·
GOD·SEND·YOU·A·HAPPY·GOD·SEND·YOU·A·HAPPY·
GOD·SEND·YOU·ALL·A·HAPPY·NEW·YEAR·
GOD·BLESS·THE·MASTER·OF·THIS·HOUSE·LIKEWISE·THE·MISTRESS·TOO
AND·ALL·THE·LITTLE·CHILDREN·THAT·ROUND·THE·TABLE·STREW

Here's to Smiler, and to her right eye,
God send our mistress a good Christmas pie ;
As good Christmas pie as e'er I did see—
With the wassailing bowl I'll drink to thee.

Here's to Fillpail, and to her long tail,
God send our master us never may fail
Of a cup of good beer ; I pray you draw near,
And our jolly wassail it's then you shall hear.

Come, butler, come, bring us a bowl of your best ;
And we hope that your soul in heaven shall rest ;
But if you do bring us a bowl of your small,
Then down shall go butler, and bowl and all.

These worldly old carols were sometimes sung to the same tunes as the religious ones. The following, " Bring us in good ale," is to be found on the same manuscript as the words of the beautiful Annunciation Carol, " Tydings true," given on page 29, and set to the same melody. This old manuscript is in the Bodleian Library at Oxford, and probably belongs to the fifteenth-century time of Henry VI. It is printed in full by the Percy Society in Wright's " Songs and Carols," where the editor says :—" The great variations in the different copies of the same song show that they were taken down from oral recitation, and had often been preserved by memory among minstrels who were not unskilful at composing, and who were not only in the habit of, voluntarily or involuntarily, modifying the songs as they passed through their hands, and adding or omitting stanzas, but of making up new songs by stringing together phrases and lines, and even whole stanzas, from the different compositions which were imprinted on their memories."

THE ANGEL GABRIEL.

Here we print the melody of " The Angel Gabriel " (in a modernised form) with the words, and also the words of the drinking song, " Bring us in good ale," adapted to the same tune.

No...el, No....el, No...el, No...el, this is the sa...lu...ta...
Good ale, Good ale, Good ale, Good ale, _ For our Bles.sed Lady's

...tion of An...gel Ga..bri...el..... Ti...dings true there be come
sake _ Bring us in good ale.... Bring us in no brown _

new, sent from the Trin...i...ty...... By Ga...bri...el to Naz.a..reth,
bread for that is made of bran.... Nor bring us in no white_ bread

Ci...ty of Ga.li...lee..... A clean maid..en, and pure Vir..gin thró her hu..
for there.in is no game... And bring us. in no beef ____ for there is

mil..i..ty..... Hath con..ceiv..ed the Per..son, Se.cond in De...i..ty.....
man.y bones... But bring us in good ale, for that go.eth down at once...

Six more stanzas follow in the " Bring us in good ale " carol dealing with bacon, mutton, tripe, eggs, butter, pork, puddings, venison, capons, and ducks, as all inferior to their " good ale " !

ANGELS AND SHEPHERDS

Perhaps none of the events of the first Christmas recorded in the Gospel story appeal more strongly to the imagination of both old and young than the appearance of the angels to the shepherds and the scene in the stable at Bethlehem. It is not surprising, therefore, to find these events a popular subject of the Carols and Mystery-Plays of the Middle Ages. Sometimes really beautiful in language, sometimes rather rough in their homely presentation, one can, nevertheless, perceive all through how earnestly the simple-minded rustics entered into the performance and enjoyment of them.

In the " Pageant of the Shearmen and Taylors " (Coventry Corpus-Christi play) there is a two-verse carol (of the " Three jolly shepherds "), which the characters acting as shepherds sing as follows :—

As I rode out this enders night,
Of three jolly shepherds I saw a sight,
And all about their fold a star shone bright ;
    They sang *terly terlow ;*
    They sang *terly terlow ;*
So merrily the shepherds their pipes can blow.

Down from heaven, from heaven so high,
Of angels there came a great company,
With mirth and joy and great solemnity,
They sang *terly terlow*,
They sang *terly terlow*,
So merrily the shepherds their pipes can blow.

The old Mystery-Plays are full of quaint legends connected with the shepherds, and there are many curious
stories of the various presents which the shepherds were
supposed to have brought as offerings to the Christ-
Child.   In the York Mysteries (about 1350) one shepherd
offers a brooch, with a little tin bell attached ; another
brought two cobnuts on a ribbon, while the third
brought a horn spoon, big enough to hold forty peas !
Then again, in the Coventry Mysteries, the first shepherd
says he can only offer his oaten pipe, " wherein much
pleasure I have found," the second shepherd offers his
hat, saying :—

" For wedder thou hast now no nede to complaine,
For wind, nor sun, hayle, snoo and rayne."

The third shepherd gives his " myttens " to keep the
Child's hands warm.

In the Towneley Plays the three shepherds bring as
their presents a bob of cherries, a bird, and a ball.

Notice the reference to the game of tennis in the following verse of the third shepherd :—

> Hail, darling dear ! full of godhead !
> I pray thee be near, when that I have need.
> Hail ! sweet is Thy cheer, my heart would bleed
> To see Thee sit here in so poor a weed
> > With no pennies. Hail ! put forth Thy dall.
> > I bring thee but a ball,
> > Have and play Thee with all,
> > And go to the tenys (tennis).

When the shepherds have presented their gifts, Mary tells how the child was born, and says :—

> > (May) He keep you from woe !
> > I shall pray Him so.
> > Tell forth as you go
> > And mind on this morn.

An old carol of the early sixteenth century, " The Jolly Shepherd Wat,"* tells very much the same story of the presents to the Christ-child. The first verse describes the " Jolly Shepherd Wat " as he sat on the hillside with

> > " His tabard and his hat,
> > His taxbox, pipe, and his flagat,
> > His name was called jolly Wat,
> > For he was a good herd's boy."

*See Miss Richert's " Ancient English Carols " for an excellent version of this old carol,

As Wat sits on the hillside he hears angels sing :
" Gloria in excelsis," and leaving his flocks and his
friends, Mall and Will, goes to Bethlehem, and finding
the Child " in a simple place, between an ox and an ass,"
he worships Him, saying :—

> " Jesu, I offer to Thee here my pipe,
> My scrip, my tax-box and my skirt ;
> Home to my fellows now will I skip,
> And also look unto my sheep."

Wat then says his farewell to St. Mary, adding,
" Lull well Jesu in thy lap, and farewell Joseph with
thy round cape ! "

> Ut hoy !
> For on his pipe he made such joy.
> Can I not sing but hoy
> When the jolly shepherd
> Made so much joy ?

In " Biographical Miscellanies," 1813, was printed
amongst others the following beautiful carol, written
about the middle of the sixteenth century, by Richard
Kele :—

> IN BETHLEHEM, THAT NOBLE PLACE.
> In Bethlehem, that noble place,
> As by the Prophets said it was,
> Of the Virgin Mary, full of grace,
> *Salvator mundi natus est.*
>> Be we merry in this feast,
>> *In quo Salvator natus est.*

The shepherds were encompassed right
About them was a wondrous light ;
" Dread ye naught," said the angel bright,
Salvator mundi natus est.
    Be we merry in this feast,
    In quo Salvator natus est.

Behold, to you we bring great joy,
And why ? for Christ is born this day ;
Find Him you with His mother may,
Salvator mundi natus est.
    Be we merry in this feast,
    In quo Salvator natus est.

And thus in faith find him ye shall,
So poorly in an ox's stall.
The shepherds then lauded God all.
Quia Salvator mundi natus est.
    Be we merry in this feast,
    In quo Salvator natus est.

EPIPHANY

As the Madonna and Child with the Angels and Shepherds supplied beautiful subjects for scenes in the Christmas mysteries of the Middle Ages, so the story of the royal kings, led from distant lands by the star to the little town of Bethlehem, and bringing their symbolical gifts of gold, frankincense, and myrrh, gave ample opportunity for religious displays of the same character. Carols and Mysteries for the Epiphany were, however, more popular on the continent of Europe than in this country, and processions and plays were common in Belgium, France, and Germany. In the British Museum there is a twelfth-century manuscript containing a miracle-play of the " Three Kings," which is included in an Epiphany-tide Processional for the use of Strasburg Cathedral, the characters of which include Herod, scribes, shepherds, and angels, as well as the three kings Gaspar, Melchior, and Balthazar. At the services in the churches the Magi were represented by curiously apparelled singers, each of whom came from a different part of the church (signifying their world-wide nationality) and met in the middle before the high altar, where they sang their carols and offered their gifts of gold, frankincense, and myrrh, to symbolize the kingship, worship, and suffering of Christ. One of the three kings was always represented as black, and to the present day the old tradition of the negro king is preserved at St. Peter's, Rome, where, on the Festival of the Epiphany, three priests say mass at three altars, and one of the priests is always a negro.

Many quaint ceremonies in connection with the " coming of the Magi " still live in Germany. Mr. Baring-Gould, in his learned preface to Chope's Carol-book, says that " in Holstein three peasants dress in white shirts—one has a black face and carries a fishing-rod with a gilt star suspended to it, and they sing a carol beginning :—

" Wir, Kaspar und Melcher, and Baltser genannt,
    Wir sind die Heiligen drei Konig aus Morgenland."

In Saxony the star is composed of oiled paper, and a lamp burns inside it. In the midst of the star a house is painted, and one of the windows is made to open by means of a string, and, like the cuckoo in a clock, a doll (Herod) pops out and bobs his head, and then retires again. This exhibition is accompanied by a curious carol, sung in parts, with question and answer, Herod popping out of his window, being supposed to be one of the singers, his part being chanted by the bearer of the star in shrill falsetto ! Mr. Baring-Gould also tells how

the dwellers in the Erz mountains in German Bohemia
march in procession through their villages. " First
goes the star, carried by the precentor ; next the Christmas Tree, hung with ribands and apples, drawn by the
rest of the players, singing sacred songs. On reaching
the hall where the miracle-play is to be performed a
semicircle is made, and a carol called the " Star-song "
is performed, beginning :—

> " In lieben meine Singer fangen tapfer an
> Zü grüssen wollen wirs heben an."

The performers then greet the sun, the moon, the
stars, the emperor, and the magistracy, in the name of
all the herbs that grow on the earth. They greet next
the master-singer and his hat, and conclude with a salutation to the constellations of Charles's Wain, the Soul-car
of German heathen mythology.

Knecht Ruprecht (the hobgoblin or devil) nearly
always accompanies these performances, and seems to
bear a family likeness to Beelzebub in the English
Mystery-Play. (See page 20.)

The following Epiphany carol is to be found both in
the British Museum and also in the Bodleian Library,
Oxford, and is of fifteenth-century origin. It will be
noticed that the English lines are made to rhyme in
couplets with the Latin.

Now make we joy in this feast,
In quo Christus natus est.

A Patre Unigenitus
Through a maid is come to us.*

Sing we of Him and say, Welcome,
Veni, Redemptor gentium.

Agnoscat omne seculum,
A bright star made three kings to come.

To seek for Him with their presents,
Verbum supernum prodiens.

Maria ventre concepit,
The Holy Ghost was ay her with.

Of her in Bethlehem born He is,
Consors Paterni luminis.

O lux beata Trinitas,
That lay between an ox and ass.

Beside His mother maiden free,
Gloria Tibi Domine.

*In another version of this carol the second line of the second stanza runs thus :—" Three young maidens came to us." The " three young maidens " are to be seen in the accompanying illustration.

A famous old English Epiphany carol, the Golden
Carol of Gaspar, Melchior, and Balthazar, is also of the
fifteenth century.

> Now is Christmas y come,
> Father and Son together in one,
> And Holy Ghost, as be all one,
> in fere-a*
> God send us a Happy New Year.
>
> I would you sing for if I might,
> Of a Child is fair in sight,
> His mother Him bare this endernight
> so still-a,
> And as it was His will-a.
>
> There came three from Galilee
> Into Bethlem, that fair citie,
> To seek for Him that e'er should be
> by right-a
> Lord and king and knight-a.
>
> Till they came into the place
> Where Jesus and His mother was.
> Offered they up with great solace
> in fere-a.
> Gold and incense and myrrh-a.

*in fere-a = together.

Forth they went these Kinges three,
Till they came home to their countrie ;
Glad they were and blythe all three
Of the sight that they had see
      by dene-a*
The company was clean-a.

*by dene-a = in company.

WELCOME TO CHRISTMAS

Christmas being a time of feasting and happiness as well as of Christian joy, our forefathers gave a right merry welcome to their Yuletide season. Naturally, when carols came to be sung in the home, as well as in the churches, it led to a large growth of carols alluding to the feasting and hospitality of the season, and we find some of them made up of an extraordinary mixture of religion and conviviality, as in the stanza given on page 118.

The following is from " Poor Robin's Almanack " for 1695, and shows how royally they feasted and made merry :—

> Now thrice welcome Christmas,
> Which brings us good cheer,
> Mince pies and plum porridge,
> Good ale and strong beer :
> With pig, goose, and capon,
> The best that can be,
> So well doth the weather
> And our stomachs agree.

Observe how the chimneys
Do smoke all about,
The cooks are providing
For dinner no doubt,
But those on whose tables
No victuals appear,
O may they keep Lent
All the rest of the year !

With holly and ivy
So green and so gay,
We deck up our houses
As fresh as the day,
With bays and rosemary,
And laurel complete :
And everyone now
Is a king in conceit.

Here is another quaint specimen—also from " Poor Robin's Almanack " for 1700 :—

Now that the time has come wherein
Our Saviour Christ was born,
The larder's full of beef and pork,
The garner's filled with corn.

While the gentlemen who sang the following must have been rather fond of the bottle :—

> And we do hope before we part
> To taste some of your beer,
> Your beer, your beer, your Christmas beer,
> That seems to be so strong ;
> And we do wish that Christmas-tide
> Was twenty times as long !

What a shock for an eighteenth-century teetotaller !

In contrast to the foregoing feasting carols, the following fifteenth-century example is restrained indeed. It will be noticed that the various Saints' days observed at Christmas-tide—Saint Stephen, Saint John, The Holy Innocents, Saint Thomas, New Year's Day, The Epiphany, or Twelfth Day (so called because it falls twelve days after Christmas), and Candlemas, or the Feast of the Purification—are all mentioned in the carol.

WELCOME YULE, THOU MERRY MAN, IN WORSHIP OF
THIS HOLY DAY.

> Welcome be Thou, heavenly King,
> Welcome, born in one morning,
> Welcome, for Whom we all sing,
> Welcome Yule.

> Welcome be ye, Stephen and John,
> Welcome, Innocents every one,
> Welcome, Thomas, martyred one,
> Welcome Yule.

Welcome be ye, good New Year,
Welcome Twelfth Day, both in fere,
Welcome Saintes lefe and dear,
    Welcome Yule.

Welcome be ye, Candlemas,
Welcome be ye, Queen of Bliss,
Welcome both to more and less,
    Welcome Yule.

Welcome be ye that are here,
Welcome all and make good cheer,
Welcome all another year,
    Welcome Yule.

A really beautiful specimen of " Welcome to Christmas " is the following, written sometime in the fifteenth
century :—

IN DIE NATIVITATIS.
" Nowell, nowell, nowell, nowell."
" Who is there that singeth so
Nowell, nowell, nowell " ?
" I am here, Sir Christemas,"
" Welcome, my lord Sir Christemas,
Welcome to all, both more and less,
    Come near Nowell."

" God be with you, Sirs, tidings I you bring ;
A maid hath borne a child full ying,
Which causeth me to sing,
    Nowell.

" Christ is now born of a pure maid,
In an ox stall He is laid,
Wherefore sing we all at abraid,
    Nowell.

Drink you all right heartily,
Make good cheer and be right merry
And sing with us now joyfully,
    Nowell."

FAREWELL
TO CHRISTMAS

When the Christmas season, with its joys and festivities was ended, and the people settled down reluctantly once more to their everyday work and habits, a natural reaction set in which found expression in the " Farewells" to Christmas. Just one specimen, with its accompanying tune, is given here to show the sort of doleful ditty which was sung to lament the passing of Christmas and its feasting and merry-making. The tune is a 16th-century melody from the " Virginal Book " of Elizabeth Rogers, and is also known as " Essex's last farewell."

CHRISTMAS HATH MADE AN END.

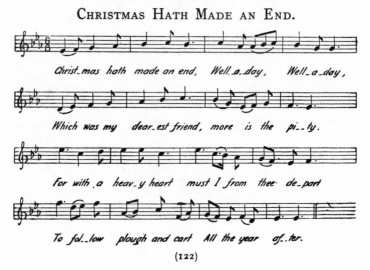

Christ-mas hath made an end, Well-a-day, Well-a-day,

Which was my dear-est friend, more is the pi--ty.

For with a heav-y heart must I from thee de-part

To fol--low plough and cart All the year af--ter.

Lent is fast coming on,
    Well-a-day, well-a-day,
That loves not anyone,
    More is the pity ;
For I doubt both my cheeks
    Will look thin eating leeks ;
Wise is he then that seeks
    For a friend in a corner.

All our good cheer is gone,
    Well-a-day, well-a-day,
And turned to a bone,
    More is the pity ;
In my good master's house
I shall eat no more souce,
Then give me one carouse,
    Gentle, kind butler.

It grieves me to the heart,
    Well-a-day, well-a-day,
From my friend to depart,
    More is the pity.
Christmas, I mean, 'tis thee
That thus forsaketh me,
Yet till one hour I see
    Will I be merry.

Thus ends this doleful ditty, together with the cessation of Christmas festivities, when the rustic returned once more to his work, and to follow the plough "all the year after," until the time came once again to recommence the merry feast of Yuletide.

THE MUSIC OF THE CAROLS

In considering the music of the carols it is well to keep in mind that many of the oldest tunes were written in the old Modal scales, which, by their peculiar tonality and the absence of chromatic intervals, give a distinctly refreshing sense of strangeness, which is fascinating to our modern ears.

These Modes were scales of eight notes, as are our present major and minor scales. Each Mode began on a different " white " note of our piano, starting with the first mode on D, another on E, and so on, but as no " accidentals " were used, except an occasional B flat, the semitones fell in each mode in different places.

The following table shows the modes and their semitones :—

D	E F	G	A	B C	D	called the	Dorian Mode
E F	G	A	B C	D	E	„	Phrygian
F	G	A	B C	D	E F	„	Lydian
G	A	B C	D	E F	G	„	Mixo lydian
A	B C	D	E F	G	A	„	Aeolian
B C	D	E F	G	A	B	„	Locrian
C	D	E F	G	A	B C	„	Ionian

While the mode of the scales was theoretically of eight notes, yet it is quite common to find a melody exceeding the range by one or more notes above or below, as in the following, which commences on the D (the first note of the mode) and descends one note lower at the second syllable of the word " Gabriel."

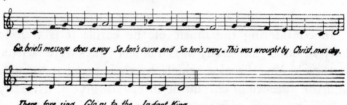

Ga.briel's message does a.way Sa.tan's curse and Sa.tan's sway. This was wrought by Christ.mas day.

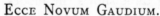

There.fore sing Glo.ry to the In.fant King.

The "Angel Gabriel" carol (see page 104) is another example of this type of melody, and is written in the second mode, transposed a fourth higher. The next illustration is an old 13th-century carol written in the seventh mode (i.e., in a scale ranging from G to G with an F natural as its seventh note). The strong effect of the F natural, a characteristic note of the seventh mode, should be noticed. The English versification is by Dr. Neale.

ECCE NOVUM GAUDIUM.

Here is joy for every age, Every ge.ne..ra.tion; Prince and pea.sant

Chief and sage, Every tongue and na.tion Every tongue and na.tion.

Every rank and sta.tion, Hath to.day Sal..va.tion. Al.le.lu......ia.

Most of the old tunes were of the Folk-song order. They were popular melodies of the times, the instinctively natural musical expression of the people themselves, and were used indiscriminately for both religious and secular words, as in the old " Angel Gabriel " carol mentioned above.

A modern example, and an excellent one, too, of an old tune adapted to carol words is the one which Sir John Stainer edited, fitted to the carol beginning :—

" What child is this, who laid to rest
In Mary's lap is sleeping " ?*

The original is a charming old English love-song, " My Lady Greensleeves " :—

My Lady Greensleeves.

A..las! my love you do me wrong to cast me off dis..courteous..ly, For

I have lov...ed you so long, de..light..ing in your com..pa..ny.

Green..sleeves was all my joy, Green..sleeves was my de..light,

Green..sleeves was my heart of gold, and all for my La...dy Green..sleeves.

*See " Christmas Carols." Novello & Co.

Very often old dance tunes were adapted to the words of carols, and in fact this was done in all countries where carols were popular. The following three examples are from the chief carol-producing countries of the Middle Ages. They are obviously all dance tunes :—

OLD GERMAN 14TH CENTURY " LIEDLEIN."

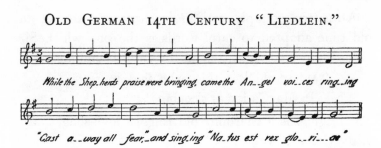

This is a " Noel de Cour " which was very popular in the sixteenth century, and sung to the carol, " Tous les bourgeois de Chartres."

While the following old English " Furry-day Song," which was sung to various sets of words relating to Christmas, May-day feasts, and other festival occasions, has such a " lilt " that one can quite easily imagine it being played by the village fiddler while the villagers danced on the green :—

Generally, these old tunes were transmitted aurally, and in the course of time often changed so much as to be entirely altered in time, tune, and character. Sir John Stainer gave some excellent examples of these changes in a lecture which he gave in Oxford in 1890. Sir John said, " Ancient church melodies were sometimes put through a curious process of transformation in order to make them suitable, or perhaps I ought to say lively enough, for carols.

Everybody knows the fine old church melody, " Conditor alme siderum " :—

K

Here is a popular version of the tune as sung to a Noel in France, and in Flanders, too :—

Here is another version from Bas-Quercy, but still more transformed :—

The first version given by Sir John Stainer is the old Plainsong melody of the Office Hymn tune for Advent, and is written in the fourth mode. Sir John might have added that Bach also used the same tune of " Conditor alme siderum " for one of his beautiful organ variations on chorales. Bach, however, gives the following version, which is more closely related to the " Sarum " or English version of the Plainsong melody :—

" Lob Sei Dem Allmachtigen Gott."

A BLESSED ANGEL.... UNTO CERTAIN
SHEPHERDS BROUGHT TIDINGS OF THE SAME

It will be gathered from the preceding remarks that carols, generally speaking, did not possess "proper" tunes, but were sung to any well-known melody which fitted them. Sometimes there was more than one tune to a popular carol, as with "God rest you, merry gentle-men," which has two, the well-known traditional version :—

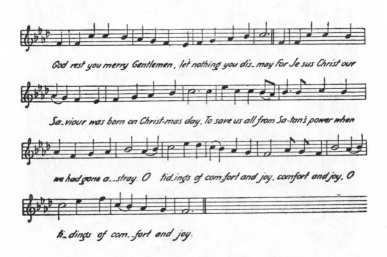

God rest you merry Gentlemen, let nothing you dis_may for Je sus Christ our

Sa_viour was born on Christ-mas day. To save us all from Sa-tan's power when

we had gone a__stray. O   tid_ings of com_fort and joy. comfort and joy. O

ti_dings of com__fort and joy.

and another traditional one, given in Mr. Sandy's collection :—

God rest you merry Gen.tle.men Let nothing you dis.may. For Je.sus

Christ our Sa.viour Was born up..on this day   O   ti..dings,

O ti..dings of comfort and of joy   For Je.sus Christ our Sa..viour

was born up.on this day.

Sometimes the words were sung to a more or less corrupted version or metamorphosed version of an old ecclesiastical melody, as the example of " Conditor alme siderum " on page 129, which, from an ancient solemn Office Hymn for Advent, became changed into a giddy little carol tune in 6-8 measures.   But from whatever source the melody is derived, it generally bears the stamp of the characteristics of the nation which used it, as can be seen by comparing the three tunes of England, France, and Germany on pages 128 and 129. The German Liedlein is very German indeed in its slow $\frac{3}{4}$ measure. The French tune is gay with the naïve gaiety of our neighbours across the Channel, while the English

" Furry-day " song is full of the " fresh air " feeling of the village green.

Much more could be written on the origin and development of carol tunes, but enough, perhaps, has been said to show what an important and interesting branch of literary and musical study lies in the subject of Carols and their Music.